THE BOOK OF ANSWERS:
The Expert's Guide to Navigating College Admissions

By
Jamie L. Reich, M.S., P.D. and Wesley Berkowitz, Ph.D.

In Association with A-List Education

THE BOOK OF ANSWERS:
The Expert's Guide to Navigating College Admissions

This book has been a labor of love and we dedicate it to the many students and families who have placed their trust in us over the years. We feel truly blessed to have had the opportunity to be invited into their lives at this exciting/daunting time of the college planning/application process. We hope that through this book we will continue to guide students and their families, past, present and future.

Heartfelt thanks to Karen Bartscherer, Jackie Nealon and Susan Miller for their indelible contributions and to Scott Reich for his commitment to this project, steadfast support and tireless efforts.

And, most of all, for the source of our inspiration and love, our families: Adam, Andrew, Beverly, Carole, Eddie, Edward, Ethan, Evelyn, Howie, Jesse, Leslie, Michael, Randi and Scott.

About the Authors

Jamie L. Reich

Jamie L. Reich, a native of Long Island, holds a Bachelor of Arts in Psychology, Sociology and Education, cum laude, from Washington University in St. Louis, Mo., a Master of Science in Education "With Distinction" with a specialization in Counselor Education from Hofstra University in Uniondale, New York as well as New York State Public School Teacher Permanent Certification in School Counseling. In addition, she holds a Professional Diploma with "High Honors" in Marriage and Family Therapy from Hofstra University.

Jamie is a Professional Member of the IECA, Independent Educational Consultants Association and is a member of NACAC, National Association for College Admission Counseling, Nassau Counselors' Association and NYSACAC, New York State Association for College Admission Counseling. Additionally, she has served as Director of College Advising Services for a prestigious New York-based education company. In an effort to remain current, she visits college campuses and meets with admission officers and academic deans on a regular basis. Jamie has successfully guided hundreds of students and their parents through the exciting, yet stressful college application process. She works closely with the student on college selection, creating a stellar resume, brainstorming essays, building interview skills, assisting with deferral/wait-list strategies as well as transfer applications. She provides early guidance for 9th, 10th and 11th graders in academic planning, extracurricular activities including community service efforts and summer planning. She also provides assistance with graduate school applications and essay brainstorming. Jamie prides herself on the trust that clients have placed in her as she becomes the "go to" person for siblings and friends. The lasting relationships she builds with clients endure well beyond the college application process.

Spending time with family and friends brings Jamie her greatest joy.

Wesley Berkowitz

Born and raised in New York City, Wesley has a Bachelor's Degree in Elementary Education/Social Science, a Masters Degree "With Distinction" in Counselor Education, a Professional Diploma in Counseling and a Family Therapy Certificate, all earned at Hofstra University in Uniondale, New York. He also has a Professional Diploma in Educational Administration from Long Island University/C.W. Post in Brookville, New York, ABD in Counseling and Guidance at Duke University in Durham, North Carolina and a Ph.D. in Counseling Psychology from The Union Institute & University in Cincinnati, Ohio.

He was a school counselor at The Wheatley School (grades 8-12) in Old Westbury, New York for 33 years, where his primary responsibilities involved personal, academic, career and college counseling. Over the course of his career, he has helped thousands of students and parents navigate the college admissions process from start to finish. His outstanding relationships with students and parents have been so positive that he is often sought out by his now-adult former students to assist their children with college admission.

Currently, he lives on the North Shore of Long Island, is happily married and the very proud father of two wonderful sons.

ADDITIONAL CONTRIBUTORS:

Karen Bartscherer, freelance writer and editor, has taught English at The Wheatley School in Old Westbury, NY and at Adelphi University in Garden City, NY.

Scott Farber is the President and co-founder of A-List Education. After graduating from Harvard University, he has overseen all aspects of the company's growth while continuing to work directly with students and schools – tutoring, training teachers, developing innovative educational products such as Vocab Videos and speaking at conferences and educational organizations across the country. Scott also co-founded CollegeEssayOrganizer.com, an online tool designed to help students streamline the college essay process, and serves in a variety of educational consulting capacities for nationally recognized non-profit programs.

Susan Miller worked for 33 years in the East Williston School District in Old Westbury, NY and is currently a special education administrator in the Locust Valley School District, Locust Valley, NY.

Dr. Jacquelyn Nealon serves as Chief of Staff and Vice President of Enrollment, Campus Life and Communications for Long Island University, Greenvale, NY. Jacquelyn is an expert in expanding college affordability, financial aid, admissions and enrollment management.

Michelle Richards attended Manhattanville College, and graduated from Hunter College with a BA in Psychology and is a member of Psi Chi, the National Honors Society in Psychology. Upon graduation Michelle started working at Graham Windham in their Therapeutic Foster Boarding Homes unit as a Sociotherapist where she worked with youth and their families providing casework counseling as well as behavior modification.

After three years in Therapeutic, Michelle transferred to Preparing Youth for Adulthood where she developed curriculum and coordinated monthly workshops on a broad range of life skills, college admissions and transitions. At A-List Education she coordinates many nonprofit partnerships, providing guidance in college selection, applications and financial aid.

Anna Marie Smith graduated from Davidson College and then served as the Associate Director of Arts nonprofit in Houston, Texas, before moving into the college admissions world. Her experience in the Office of Admission at Rice University and New York University includes reviewing undergraduate applications, recruiting students and conducting admission interviews for prospective students. In addition to working as the Chief of Staff and Director of College Advising at A-List, Anna Marie recently completed her MFA in Design Criticism from the School of Visual Arts.

Edward Smallwood is a founding partner of A-List Education, and has recently brought the expertise and excellence of its US operations to the European market, while serving as President of A-List UK. Ed passed through the British education system, attending Harrow School before moving to the US to study as an undergraduate at Harvard University. He has subsequently received his Masters from New York University and holds an MBA from Columbia Business School and London Business School.

Mark Kowalsky is a college counselor at the Schechter School of Long Island, having educated teenagers and their families for almost 41 years. A former high school English teacher at Forest Hills High School, Guidance Counselor at The Wheatley School in Long Island's East Williston School District, from where he retired after fourteen years, and college admissions counselor for New York Institute of Technology, Mark brings a wealth of experience and expertise to the college admissions process. He holds a BA in English from CUNY Brooklyn College, an MA in English Education from New York University and an MS in School Counseling from St. John's University. He has certification in administration from New York University and has extensive coursework and experience in art history, a field which inspires him as his students continue to enrich his life. He is actively involved in many professional organizations and college admissions conferences. Mark has visited hundreds of colleges throughout his long career, built a network of colleagues and college admissions counselors and as a result, has kept abreast of all components of the college process.

INTRODUCTION
AND A NOTE OF CAUTION

There are many college books on the market today, but unfortunately, most tend to be bulky and not user friendly when it comes to answering questions about applying to college. We decided to write a book that speaks directly to you, the parent, about the nuts and bolts of what to expect, and to help navigate the many facets of the college admission process.

Over the years, parents and students have consistently asked us the kinds of questions that are neither typically nor readily found in most college books. Our handbook is a compilation of answers to the most often asked questions as each step of applying to college unfolds. Every chapter covers an important component of the process, and provides answers in an easy to understand format. It is a single all-in-one resource that offers a compendium of information that catalogs the subject matter, enabling readily accessible answers.

While we endeavor to provide as much current information and clarity as possible, there is no substitute for following up with particular colleges to ensure accurate deadlines and requirements. We cannot guarantee that everything contained in this book is 100% accurate as each admissions season brings change, but we can promise that this work is a valuable starting point as you try to navigate the college admissions process.

CONTENTS

What do the SAT and ACT actually test and what's the difference between the two?

We are sure you've heard all sorts of things about this—things like: The ACT is more like the stuff students learn in school and the SAT tries to trick you! Or, the ACT is easier! Or, the SAT is easier!

Here is the truth: The SAT and the ACT are very similar exams as they both combine content learned in school with reasoning abilities.

Parents and students are often told that the ACT is more aligned with classroom learning and tests than the old format SAT. The fact that the ACT contains a "science" section contributes to a good portion of misinformation. The section itself is approximately 95% data interpretation—similar to a reading passage. A test-taker might encounter 1-2 questions on the science section that won't be answered in the passages, but the majority of the information is right in the test. The new SAT has categories for analysis in science and history/social science, which will also appear to be more "content" aligned. The truth is that the tests are incredibly similar and generally test the same skill sets.

•

Should my son/daughter consider the ACT, since the SAT is changing?

The SAT is changing in March 2016.

According to the College Board, the test will better reflect high school curriculum and be a better indicator of college readiness.

In general, it's not that we recommend one test over the

other, but as colleges look to both tests equally, your child should consider the well-established ACT as an alternative to the new SAT.

	Old SAT Format (until January 2016)
Scoring	2400 total points: Math, Critical Reading and Writing scores will each range between a 200-800; Composite SAT score is the sum of the three scores, ranging from 600-2400.
Differences in Format	**10 sections total:** • Critical Reading: Two 25-min sections and one 20-min section. • Math: Two 25-min sections and one 20-min section. One of the 25-min sections includes 10 non-multiple choice questions. • Writing: One 25-min essay, one 25-min section and one 10-min section. • Equating: One 25-min section in Critical Reading, Math or Writing (does not count in your final score).
Is there a penalty for wrong answers?	Yes – Wrong answers on multiple choice questions cost 1/4 of a point.
Do you get Score Choice?	The College Board offers Score Choice. However, many colleges will request all of your scores. It's always best to check the college websites to be sure.
Difficulty Levels	Questions increase in difficulty level as you move through that question type in a section (except read- ing passage questions, which progress chronologically through the passage).
Math Levels	Arithmetic, Data Analysis, Algebra I and II, Functions, and Geometry. **Some Formulas Provided**

	New SAT Format (starting March 2016)
Scoring	1600 total points: Math, Reading, and Writing scores will each range between a 200-800; Composite SAT score (including the optional essay) is the sum of the three scores, ranging from 400-1600
Differences in Format	**5 sections total** (including optional essay): • <u>Evidence-Based Reading & Writing</u>: One 65-min section and one 35-min section • Reading: 65-min section • Writing and Language: 35-min section • <u>Math</u>: One 55-min section and one 35-min section. • No Calculator: 25-min section • Calculator OK: 55-min section • <u>Essay (Optional)</u>: 50-min
Is there a penalty for wrong answers?	No
Do you get Score Choice?	The College Board offers Score Choice. However, many colleges will request all of your scores. It's always best to check the college websites to be sure.
Difficulty Levels	Questions increase in difficulty level as you move through that question type in a section.
Math Levels	Content heavily weighted towards Algebra (62% of the test), Problem Solving and Data Analysis including percentile, ratios, and statistics (28%), and Geometry and Trigonometry (only 10%).

	ACT
Scoring	36 total composite points: English, Math, Reading and Science Reasoning scores will each range from 1-36. Composite ACT score is the average of your scores on the four sections; ranges between 1-36.
Differences in Format	5 sections total (including optional essay): • <u>English</u>: 45-min section • <u>Math</u>: 60-min section • <u>Reading</u>: 35-min section • <u>Science</u>: 35-min section • <u>Writing</u>: 30-min section (optional)
Is there a penalty for wrong answers?	No
Do you get Score Choice?	The ACT offers Score Choice but many colleges will request all of your scores. You do have the option with the ACT to remove an entire test date from your record.
Difficulty Levels	The math section questions are in order of difficulty; the other sections are more randomized.
Math Levels	Arithmetic, Algebra I and II, Functions, Geometry, and Trigonometry. **No formulas provided upfront, some may be included in the questions**

How was the old format SAT scored and was there a "curve"?

SAT scores are in a 200–800 point scale, and it seems like each question is worth a different number of points, so there is an obvious question: why?

Each time they gave the SAT, they used a new test form. But they wanted the scores to be standard across all students on all dates (thus the phrase "standardized test"). No matter how hard they tried, there were always slight variations in the difficulty level of each test form; this one was slightly harder or slightly easier than the last one. So instead of just counting up how many rights and wrongs students got, they converted performance to a scaled score of 200-800. Each test had its own scoring table that adjusts for the difficulty of the test. If a particular test form was harder than usual, the scoring table was be more generous, and a given number of right answers would have given your child a slightly higher score. If a form was easier than usual, the scoring table would have been harsher, and the same number of right answers would have given a slightly lower score.

This was all done to ensure that a final SAT score was not affected by the date a student happened to take the test.

•

What is the new SAT?

The SAT has recently undergone some radical changes starting in March 2016. This of course means that there isn't as much official practice material available, and consequently not as much data we can analyze. Since everything is so new, there's still a chance the College Board (the people who make the SAT) might surprise us. We've combined the information that has been released with our knowledge of and experience with the SAT's history to allowed us to get a firm grasp of what will be expected of your child. As more information is released and more tests are given, we'll be able to make a deeper analysis of past exams and firmer predictions about how to maximize your child's preparation for the test.

•

How is the new format SAT (starting March 2016) scored?

One of the more noticeable changes to the SAT in 2016 is that the scoring system is more complicated:

- On each of the two sections—Evidence-Based Reading & Writing and Math—your child will get a section score from 200 to 800.

- These two section scores will be added together to give students a total score from 400 to 1600.

- For each of the three tests—Reading, Writing, and Math—your son/daughter will get a test score from 10 to 40.

The section scores and test scores are the most important ones. This is confusing so let us explain. In general, scores are calculated by taking the number of right answers (the "raw score"), and translating that score into a final number using a special scoring table. Each test has its own unique scoring table in order to adjust for differences among tests: a harder test will be more slightly generous about awarding points.

However, the Math section uses a lookup table for its section score, while the Reading and Writing sections use lookup tables for their test scores.

The Evidence-Based Reading and Writing section (we'll call it EBRW) is made up of two parts called Tests, as we saw in the table above. For each of these tests, you add up the number of right answers and use a special table to find a student's Test Score, 10 to 40. Then you add the Reading Test score and Writing Test score, multiply by 10, and that's your child's EBRW Section score. Let's say your son/daughter got a 23 on the Reading Test and a 25 on the Writing test; add them together and multiply by 10 to get a 480 on the EBRW section.

$23 + 25 = 48$ $48 \times 10 = 480$.

The Math section works the other way around. The Math ection is also made up of two parts (calculator and no calculator), but you don't get separate scores for those parts. The Math section is the Math Test. You add up all of the correct answers on both Math sections and use a special table to find the section score, 200- 800. Then you divide by 10 and divide by 2 to get your Math Test score. You get an 800-point score and a 40-point score for the same set of 58 questions. Why? Who knows! Symmetry, we guess.

•

What are the new cross-test and subscores on the SAT?

Your child will get 18 scores showing his/her performance on different types of questions within a single SAT test. For example, *Heart of Algebra* is a subscore in the Math section. There are also cross-test scores showing a student's performance across different sections, such as *Analysis in History/Social Science*, which is drawn from math, reading, and writing questions. At this point, no one is certain how important each of these scores will be to colleges, so don't worry about them too much and encourage your child to remain focused on the 1600 point scale.

•

I heard the May test is easier than the March test. Is it true?

There is no such thing as "the easy test date." There are some urban legends floating around about how the May test is easier or the March test is harder. None of these rumors are true. A score is **not** based on the performance of the other students on a particular test date.

The test is administered and designed by very bright and seasoned individuals; people with Ph.D.'s in statistics who understand Math in ways most of us can't even begin to imagine. They have anticipated objections, and they go through great lengths to ensure that all test dates produce equivalent scores.

Both the ACT and the SAT go to painstaking lengths to ensure that each test is of the same measured difficulty. The number of seniors vs. juniors also makes no difference—the curve isn't a normal curve like the tests taken in school.

The test makers do everything they can to make sure that scores are as accurate as possible.

•

What is the PSAT/NMSQT?

The PSAT is practice for the SAT. It's basically a shorter version of the SAT. Students have three opportunities to take the PSAT:

1. In 8th or 9th grade, students may take the PSAT 8/9, which is an abbreviated version of the PSAT.

2. In 10th grade, students may take the PSAT 10. This is identical to the PSAT given to juniors.

3. In 11th grade, students may take the PSAT/ NMSQT. Almost all juniors will take the PSAT.

Is the PSAT helpful in the college application process?

Though some high schools require it, the PSAT is typically optional. However, even though it's optional, taking the PSAT is a great idea. It gives all students the opportunity to practice in a real testing situation and provides an accurate sense of a starting score. You'll also receive detailed feedback on your child's strengths and weaknesses in December. Students should thoroughly review the Score Report for questions they missed. There's no pressure: if a student does poorly, it doesn't matter—colleges never see these scores.

The Preliminary SAT/National Merit Scholarship Qualifying Test (PSAT/NMSQT) serves as an initial screen of more than 1.5 million entrants each year for the National Merit Program. It also provides a valuable assessment of your child's strengths and weaknesses in Evidence-Based Reading and Writing, and Math. These results will help to identify the specific areas on which to concentrate for optimal results and will guide the SAT preparation. By taking the test in 11th grade and by meeting published participation standards, your child will qualify to enter scholarship competitions. (Note: Taking the PSAT in 10th grade does not count towards scholarship competitions and is primarily used as practice to familiarize students with the test content under timed conditions).

Of the entrants, approximately 50,000 with the highest PSAT/ NMSQT Selection Index scores in critical reading, math and writing skills qualify for recognition and will be contacted through their schools as either a Commended Student or Semifinalist. The determining factor between the two categories is based on a nationally applied Selection Index score and varies from year to year. In September of the senior year, more than two-thirds of the 50,000 high scorers will receive Letters of

Commendation in recognition of outstanding promise but do not continue in the competition for National Merit Scholarships. These students may, however, become candidates for Special Scholarships sponsored by businesses.

About 16,000 students are Semifinalists and are notified that they are the highest scoring entrants on a state-by-state basis. They are required to fill out a scholarship application from NMSC to be considered for a National Merit Scholarship and must meet high academic standards among other requirements to advance to Finalist standings. Approximately 15,000 Semifinalists will be notified through their high school in February of senior year informing them of their advancement to the Finalist level. They will be presented with a Certificate of Recognition.

From the Finalist group, winners of the Merit Scholarship awards are chosen based on a number of additional qualifications: skills, abilities, leadership and accomplishments, academic record, school profile information regarding grading system, test scores, recommendation from a high school official and the Finalist's personal essay. Some 8300 Finalist awards are announced beginning in March and continuing through June of the senior year in high school.

They fall into one of the following three categories: National Merit $2500 Scholarships, Corporate-sponsored and College-sponsored Merit Scholarship awards.

National Merit $2500 Scholarships are awarded on a state-by- state basis and are selected regardless of family finances, college choice or career plans.

Corporate-sponsored Merit Scholarships are awarded for Finalists who fall into one of three categories:

children of their employees or members, residents of a community where a company has operations or students who have career plans that the corporation wants to promote. This may be in the form of a one-time award or one that is renewable for the four years of undergraduate school.

College-sponsored merit Scholarship awards are offered to accepted students who have indicated that the particular college is their first choice. These awards are renewable for up to four years of undergraduate study.

Finally, taking the PSAT/NMSQT exam automatically includes a student in the Student Search Service, a data base system that colleges use to identify and contact prospective students whom they consider to be good matches for their schools.

•

How is the PSAT different from the SAT?

The PSAT is an abbreviated version of the SAT. The former can make your child eligible for scholarships, but it's the latter that colleges are interested in.

The SAT contains some math concepts that students are expected to learn during junior year of high school. Since the PSAT is given at the beginning of junior year, the test makers realize that not everyone has learned these concepts yet and don't include them. So the SAT will have some additional concepts, such as higher-level function problems, more graphing and some absolute value.

SAT and PSAT scores are calibrated to each other. That means your child can expect that his/her PSAT score is roughly the same as what he/she would get on the SAT if they took it the same day.

Many students naturally will do better on the SAT than the PSAT, both because they've learned more and because they've had more practice.

•

Do colleges consider the ACT to be inferior, equal, or superior to the SAT?

The SAT and ACT are regarded equally by colleges and universities and are virtually interchangeable. Some colleges will use the ACT Plus Writing in lieu of both the SAT and the SAT Subject Tests. As of this publication date, a number of schools do this: Amherst College, Barnard College, Boston College, Brandeis University, Brown, Bryn Mawr, Case Western Reserve, Connecticut College, Duke, Franklin and Marshall, Hamilton, Johns Hopkins, McGill, Middlebury, Pomona, Rensselaer Polytechnic, Swarthmore, Trinity, Tufts, Union, University of Pennsylvania, University of Richmond. If your child scores better on one of the tests, then there is no need to submit the scores on the other. If your child scores equally well on the SAT and the ACT, you should consider submitting both scores to schools to demonstrate consistency.

•

Should my child take the PSAT in 10th grade or wait until 11th grade?

There are mixed views on this question. If the PSAT is viewed strictly for what it is, a practice test and nothing more, then it can be considered. However, taking the test just two months into the sophomore year of high school means your child will not have the benefit of the natural learning curve that typically occurs between

---

[1] Of course, this does NOT mean that your child will automatically improve from his or her PSAT score without doing any work. There is a lot of variation between individuals. Only about 55% of students improve their scores on each individual section from the PSAT to the SAT.

10th and 11th grades.[1] Also, ordinarily, 10th graders have not sufficiently covered some mathematics topics so early in the school year to demonstrate proficiency on the test.

There are additional concerns to weigh, as well. Strong PSAT scores in 10th grade may cause some students to become too self-assured, possibly leading to a cavalier attitude toward preparation for the actual SAT the following year. Or suppose a student does not do very well? Will this cause unnecessary anxiety about the test simply because it was attempted too soon? Keep in mind that only the test scores from 11th grade are used for scholarship program competitions, the decision of whether to take the PSAT in 10th grade should, at the very least, be considered carefully.

•

Should my child take the ACT or the ACT Plus Writing?

The ACT Plus Writing is strongly recommended. A small percentage of schools do not require it, but the vast majority of them do. Taking the test with the Writing section ensures that your child will meet all necessary requirements if applying to even one school that requires it.

•

Is it a good idea to take both the SAT and the ACT?

It is best for the student to take one or two diagnostic tests for both the SAT and the ACT to determine which test works best for your child, taking into account many factors including timing. Your child can then focus on preparing for the test that fits best. Depending on your child's score, he or she might opt to re-take that same standardized test to increase the score. Together with your child and school advisor, you can come to a decision about which test makes the most sense.

•

What's the latest my child should take the SAT? ACT? SAT Subject Tests?

Your child should take the SAT and/or ACT in the fall/ winter or spring of junior year, if possible, and retake whichever test offers the better score opportunity in the fall of senior year. Generally, students take the SAT in March or May of their junior year and a second time in October or November of senior year. The ACT could also be taken in the spring of junior year, and if your child wishes to take it a second time, should try to do so in September or October of senior year. Bear in mind that if your child is applying to college Early Decision or Early Action, it is recommended that the final standardized test should be taken six weeks prior to the college application deadline for the individual decision plans ensuring there is sufficient time to receive the scores and report them to the colleges.

Ideally, the Subject Tests should be taken immediately upon completion of an Honors or AP course in that specific subject, when the knowledge is freshest in the student's memory.

Obviously, this would render the best chance for success on the Subject Tests, without much additional preparation. Good performance on these tests will demonstrate the skills acquired in the respective areas. Colleges often use these tests upon enrollment to place your child out of lower level courses.

•

How many times should my child take the SAT or ACT?

Unless your child achieves spectacular scores on the first try, it makes sense to take the SAT and/or the

ACT again. Many students are able to improve their performance with a second attempt. However, research indicates that taking the test more than twice does not significantly increase the overall score. Nevertheless, if there is one particular component that consistently remains your child's Achilles' heel, taking it again to reach a desired score makes a lot of sense.

•

How does "superscoring" work?

Superscoring of standardized tests is used by some colleges whereby the scores from different test dates are combined, taking into account the highest score of each section within the SAT and ACT, respectively, regardless of test date. It is a policy of many (but not all) colleges to use a student's best test scores on each section of both the SAT and ACT (whichever one your child opts to submit for admission criteria) from multiple test administrations to arrive at the best possible composite score. Many schools require submission of all scores, but their computers will typically kick out the lowest scores of each section by test date, considering the highest scores as representative of true capability.

To give you a better understanding of superscoring the ACT, if your child took the test on two sittings and scored a 30 on English, 27 on Math, 30 on Reading and 27 on Science on the first sitting and a 30 on English, 29 on Math, 30 on Reading and 28 on Science on the second sitting, the 29 Math score from the second sitting would replace the 28 Math score from the first sitting and the 28 in Science from the second sitting would replace the 27 from the first sitting. Your child would then have an improved composite score. On the SAT, if your child scores a 710 on the Math section in the first sitting and a 780 on the second, colleges that superscore the SAT will combine the 780 with the best

Critical Reading and Writing scores.

•

Do colleges superscore both the SAT and ACT?

It depends on the policy of each individual school. At the time of this publication, here is a list of some schools that superscore the ACT: Amherst College, Annapolis, Babson College, Boston College, Brandeis University, Brown University, Caltech, Colby College, Connecticut College, Middlebury College, New York University, Pomona College, Tufts University, University of Chicago, Washington University (MO) and Wesleyan University, to name a few. Other colleges will use the highest subscores on the ACT, but will not change the composite – or "superscore."

For information about how specific colleges score the SAT, go to: professionals.collegeboard.com/profdownload/sat-score-use-practices-list.pdf. It is best to research the admissions criteria directly from each school's website to get the most current information.

What is the difference between superscoring and Score Choice?

Score Choice enables students to choose specific test dates they want to submit to colleges. If your child took the SAT four times, he or she could choose to send only one or two of those dates' scores to the colleges instead of the four scores, which many schools require. With superscoring, your child can send specific scores rather than entire tests.

Both superscoring and Score Choice are optional. It is best to check the college websites to be certain that the school offers these options.

•

I heard that some schools don't even require the SAT or ACT?

Some schools are "Test Optional" which means that students can choose not to submit standardized tests if they feel their scores don't adequately reflect their abilities. If a students chooses this option, he/she may need to submit a graded school paper or take a personal interview so that the school has another means of assessment. One thing to take into account is that some schools may require test scores for scholarship consideration, even if they do not use scores for admissions purposes.

Some schools are "Test Flexible" which means that students can fulfill testing requirements by sending SAT or ACT scores or by sending SAT Subject Test scores, a combination of AP scores, etc.

For more information on "Test Optional" and "Test Flexible" schools, visit www.fairtest.org.

•

What are the most important criteria in college admissions?

The college admissions process is an art, not a science. Admission officers weigh many criteria: test scores, GPA, letters of recommendation, extracurricular activities, the required and supplemental college essays and interviews (when recommended). Additionally, a number of colleges take geographic location into account. Depending on the school, GPA and test scores have a significant impact and offer an indication of how ready the student is for college and how well a student will be able to handle the academic rigor of college classes. Even so, leadership and community involvement can play a major role. Admission officers want to see how a student is involved in the community in high school and what that student will bring to the college campus. This is a great question to ask during campus tours and information sessions.

•

What are the components of my child's college application file?

Your child's guidance counselor will submit a high school transcript, school profile and a letter of recommendation. In addition, many schools will require recommendations from teachers (usually two). Increasingly, colleges require that teacher and guidance counselor recommendations be submitted through Naviance, if the school uses this software. Your child is responsible for submitting the completed application with all required essays, application fees and resume (if required). Your child must report standardized test scores directly from www.act.org or the SAT from www.collegeboard.com.

•

What is the difference between the Common Application and the Universal College Application?

The nonprofit organization behind the Common Application offers a standard application form that is accepted by more than 550 colleges and universities. This application enables students to complete personal data and upload a personal statement essay once, yet submit this information to multiple colleges.

Your child should go to www.commonapp.org and follow the prompts to create an account with his/her email and password.

The for-profit Universal College Application is accepted by more than 40 colleges and universities and was also created to save time for students by enabling them to submit the same application to any of the participating colleges. Most of the schools participating in the Universal College Application also accept the Common Application.

•

My child is having a problem with his/her Common Application. Is there someone they can contact for help?

There is no phone support available. All technical support is done by email through the Help Center which is located on the Common Application itself. (Note: Add this address to your child's address book so tech support responses will not go to the SPAM folder: appsupport@commonapp.org) Manyquestions can be answered directly through links on the Applicant Help Center and related searches on the Knowledgebase tab. These can be reached from a button on the commonapp. org homepage.

• • •

Does my child really need to have a resume?

While many colleges do not require students to submit resumes, it can be helpful, especially if your child is applying to the more and most competitive colleges. In one organized, succinct document, your child can share detailed information about academic honors, awards, extracurricular activities, private lessons, work experience, travel, community service and other appropriate events. Some interviewers will use information from the resume as an icebreaker during an alumni or on-campus interview.

Please note that a resume will only supplement, not replace, the Activities Section of the Common Application. Students can use the Additional Information section of the Common Application (underneath Writing) to elaborate activities of importance or to cut and paste a resume. Some colleges may allow for an upload of a resume in their individual Questions sections.

•

What's the best format to use for the resume?

A resume should be no longer than two pages. Topics should be in bold type, and items within each category should be listed in chronological order. Admission officers want to see the hours/ week and weeks/year that your child was involved, so include those as well.

•

What makes a resume stand out?

An especially strong GPA or standardized test scores, although noted on other documents, are worth repeating on a resume. Also, any title in a school or community organization (i.e. president, captain, treasurer) that has been earned should be listed in bold font. Any special talents recognized in or out of school are important highlights to feature on a resume as well. Finally, any summer activities of substance (i.e. taking college courses, community service) should also be detailed. As with every other document sent to a prospective college, make sure spelling and grammar are perfect!

•

Is there anything not to list on a resume?

Any brief or superficial activities should not be listed. For example, colleges are not interested in knowing that your son/ daughter likes playing handball in the summer, watching action movies, or playing video games. Colleges are interested in substance, not fluff.

•

Are social security numbers required on the resumes?

A social security number is not necessary, and listing it could make your child vulnerable to identity theft. With date of birth, email address, home address and phone number listed on the resume, there's more than enough identifying information should the document inadvertently become separated from the rest of the application.

• • •

What is the difference between Early Action, Restrictive Early Action (also called Single-Choice Early Action) and Early Decision?

Early Decision: ED is an optional plan offered by many colleges in which students make a commitment to a first-choice institution where, if admitted, they definitely will enroll. While pursuing admission under an Early Decision plan, students may apply to other institutions, but may have only one Early Decision application pending at any time. Early Decision deadlines are usually November 1 (some schools are October 15 and November 15) and decisions are released in mid-December. This is a binding decision/contract that is signed by the student (and parent) at the time of the application. If admitted, all other applications that have been submitted must be withdrawn. Obviously, careful research, campus visits, interviews, financial factors and satisfactory completion of standardized tests prior to application are critical.

Early Action: For colleges offering this option, students apply by November 1 (some schools are November 15) and receive decision notification between mid-December and mid-January. Early Action is not a binding contract; however, students should thoroughly research all of the educational opportunities offered, visit campuses, take alumni or on-campus interviews, complete SAT and/or ACT with Writing tests and consider financial factors prior to applying Early Action.

Single-Choice or Restrictive Early Action: Applications must be submitted prior to November 1 and decisions are rendered in mid-December. This is a non-binding decision plan; however, students should have thoroughly and carefully researched all of their educational options, visited campuses, taken interviews, completed all standardized testing and considered financial factors prior to applying.

The student cannot apply Early Action or Early Decision to any other private institutions; however, application to public institutions or colleges outside the United States, provided that admission is not binding, is acceptable. Certain schools that utilize this decision plan have additional requirements on applications, and it is your child's obligation to understand the specifics pertaining to each of his/her colleges.

The student may apply to an Early Decision II program after receiving a decision from the Single-Choice Early Action program. If admitted through another college's Early Decision II binding program, your child must withdraw the application from the Single-Choice Early Action school.

Early Decision II: This option refers to those colleges who offer two Early Decision opportunities. While the deadline for ED I is typically November 1st or 15th, the deadline for ED II is usually in early to mid-January. ED II is for students who either fall in love with a school past the ED I deadline, or were deferred or denied from their first choice college, and the ED II college is now their new first choice. ED II also benefits students who are late bloomers by allowing the college to view their midyear grades before making a decision.

•

If my child applies Early Decision (ED) or Early Action (EA) to a college, should he/she send them first quarter grades?

Yes, if one of these three conditions apply:

- the college requires them

- the student maintains a strong academic profile
- a student has improved upon past performance

•

Is there a benefit to applying EA or ED?

Statistics demonstrate that a higher percentage of students who apply ED or EA are accepted to the incoming freshman class. That being said, the applicant pool is different, since these students are committing to attend, if they are admitted. Acceptance rates vary year to year depending on the number of applicants and the strength of the pool. Most schools do not have a quota for any of their decision plans, so the applicant's strengths and quality of application are more important than the choice of decision plan. One reason schools admit more students in ED or EA is that it will increase their matriculation rate, which reflects well on their admission statistics. The most important consideration must always be whether the university is your child's absolute top choice, and if accepted your child is ready to make a commitment to enroll.

•

What does it mean to be "deferred"?

An applicant can only be deferred in Early Action and Early Decision. This means that the admissions committee has not made a decision about acceptance yet; your child remains in the applicant pool for reconsideration during the review of applications for regular admissions. If your child is deferred, any significant new information should be reported to the Undergraduate Admissions office in an effort to enhance your child's chances of ultimately being accepted, including awards received, new employment or community service endeavors and new positions/titles held in activities in or out of school. Many schools will request midyear grades before making an admissions decision and even after an offer of admission has been made. These current senior grades can make or break an admissions decision. Students must inform their school counselor when these documents are requested. In addition, keeping in touch with an admission officer and confirming that the school is still the top choice will only benefit the student's application.

•

What is Rolling Admission?

Rolling Admission enables the student to submit an admissions application at any time. The institutions will process all credentials at the time they are received, without regard to a specific application due date. An admissions decision is then typically rendered within a 4-10 week period.

•

What is Regular Decision?

Regular Decision generally refers to the traditional admissions timetable. Typically, students submit their applications and supporting documents by January 1st or 15th and will receive an admissions decision in early to mid-April.

•

Some schools have Priority Admission Deadlines. What are these?

Some schools indicate that, in order to be considered for scholarships and honors programs, students must submit applications by a deadline that is earlier than their traditional deadlines. For example, if you apply by November 1 to the University of Maryland, you will automatically be considered for their Honors Programs. Check admissions deadline timetables on the school's website.

•

What does it mean to be "waitlisted"?

Waitlists refer specifically to regular and rolling decision plans. Colleges and universities will postpone making a final decision about some potentially admissible candidates. Once the school has received notifications from admitted students who, by accepting offers at other colleges, have created openings for students on their waitlists, the colleges and universities revisit their waitlisted students and make their final decisions about these candidates. While some waitlists are ranked, others are not. If a school overenrolled one year, they may waitlist and later admit those students the following year in order to keep their matriculate numbers on target. There is no definite way to know if a school will take students off a waitlist each year. Some schools, especially the most selective, may not even go to their waitlist.

•

If my child is waitlisted, what can be done to strengthen the application?

If the desire to attend the school is serious and strong, keep the admissions officer well informed and confirm that your child will attend if admitted. Additionally, your child must continue to keep strong grades and report any and all positive tidbits of information that have occurred since the application was filed. It won't hurt to arrange another campus visit, perhaps even interview with an on-campus admissions officer and sit in on classes. All of these extras demonstrate to the college a clear commitment and interest.

•

Can my child appeal a denial decision?

Only some schools allow you to appeal a denial. Your child can appeal a denial by substantiating any new information that has occurred since the application was submitted. It is a very difficult process to win, but if being admitted to a particular college is very important, it might be worth giving it a shot. Realistically, however, students should consider looking more carefully at the colleges to which have already been offered acceptances because perhaps there are untapped alternatives to their "dream" school.

•

What happens if my child gets accepted Early Decision, and decides later to attend another college. Is there any penalty?

When an ED application is filed, a binding contract is entered into with the school, stating that if admission is granted, your child will attend. Your child cannot back out of this contract after applying to a school Early Decision. This is precisely why your child needs to think long and hard BEFORE making an ED application.

•

My student's favorite college doesn't offer Early Decision. How does my child let them know they're the #1 choice and will attend if admitted?

Your child should let them know on the application supplement. Your child may also email the admissions office informing them of your child's intentions. It would be more personal if your child sent an email to the regional admissions officer. If your child cannot find out who the regional admission officer is, email the school and ask to have the letter added to the application file.

• • •

How many colleges should my child apply to?

In most cases, about eight colleges is a good number, including safety, target and reach schools. A safety school is one in which your child's GPA and standardized test scores are well above the publicized admission criteria. A target school is one to which your child has a 50/50 shot of acceptance, and where a student's GPA and standardized test scores are within the requirements of the school for acceptance. A reach school is exactly that...a reach. Taking a realistic reach is a good move. There are certainly other factors that come into play for admission, especially if your child is on the cusp for admission. They include high school activities, leadership roles, teacher recommendations and, of course, essays. If there is a wide discrepancy between the math and reading sections of your child's standardized tests, he/she should probably apply to more than ten schools to give him/herself the broadest range of possibilities for acceptance.

•

Is the deadline for applying the postmark date or the actual date?

Since colleges now expect applications to be submitted online (unless otherwise indicated on the application), the deadline is obviously the actual date, at 11:59 PM YOUR local time. For applications that must be sent through the mail, play it safe and assume that the application must be received by the college by the stated due date.

•

Should my child work with a private counselor, or is a school counselor a good option?

It all depends. Is your child a motivated, self-starter, who will utilize the services offered by the high school? For instance, does he/she plan to ask an English teacher to proofread and critique the college essays? If that's going to be the strategy, then it's unlikely that a private counselor will be needed. However, if your child feels either insecure or overwhelmed or both, the extra support provided by a private college counselor in navigating the college admissions process may well be worth the investment.

An independent educational consultant or college advisor is a valued resource for applicants and parents who want a more individualized, personal and caring approach to the highly stressful college planning and application process. So much of finding the right "fit" for the applicant involves spending the time to really get to know a student and get a handle on what might be the right college setting. Independent educational consultants have insight into the colleges because they spend a considerable amount of time touring campuses and their surrounding area and meeting with admissions officers. Additionally, they regularly attend conferences and workshops to remain current in new trends. As a result, private college advisors provide assistance with clients by providing objective advice throughout the entire college application process.

•

Should my child fill out the Common Application ("Common App") or use the school's individual application?

If applying to a Common Application member school, your child should use the Common App. If a school offers both the Common App and its own application, it will not have a preference for either application type, but choosing to use the Common App for as many schools as possible will keep students from duplicating efforts.

•

Should my child send in any supplemental information?

Any additional writing samples, resumes, or graded papers that a college or university may want, they will request as uploaded documents in the Writing Supplement of the Common Application. Additionally, if new information about your child becomes available at any time (i.e. awards, position of leadership), he/she should certainly be sure to inform the colleges about it. Keeping in touch demonstrates continued interest in attending that school.

•

My child has submitted the Common Application and wants to make a change. Is it possible?

On the Common Application, you can make unlimited edits to an already submitted application and before the second is submitted with the exception of the 650 word maximum essay. This essay should not be tailored to one specific school, as those supplemental essays will be found on the Writing Supplement of the Common Application. If your child has major changes to an application that needs to be updated, it is possible to email the new document to the school and ask to have it uploaded to the application.

•

How does a school's weighting of grades factor into the GPA?

Many high schools have different weighting systems, and others do not weight at all. Along with the transcript, the guidance counselor will send a high school profile describing the courses that your child took and the weighting system. Colleges have a method by which they determine how to equalize grading systems to accommodate the differences. Since some schools do not recalculate GPAs, they will look to see if your child has taken the most difficult classes offered.

•

Will home schooling help or hurt my child's chances for being accepted to colleges?

Nearly 1% of students living in the United States are home schooled. Because admissions policies vary from school to school, college-bound students must understand the individual requirements of each school to which they intend to apply. Deadlines must be adhered to and a detailed account of your child's academic coursework must be prepared for submission. As a home-schooled student, your child is required to verify academic expertise through standardized tests: the SAT I, ACT and SAT Subject Tests. Additionally, your child must submit evaluations from someone other than you, the parent, even if you are the primary instructor. Leadership and community service efforts are important components of your child's application.

•

What is a gap year?

A gap year is an intermission from traditional education. It usually refers to a student taking time off between graduating from high school and entering college. It is a time to gain life experience and maturity in a setting other than the academic environment. This may be done in a structured environment and awakens the learning process in a different venue. While this can be a positive experience, the lag in educational continuity can sometimes result in finding it difficult to get back into a frame of mind conducive to an educational setting. Most students taking a gap year after graduation will apply to colleges before graduating, and then defer admission for a year. (Not all schools allow a student to defer, so check with the colleges to learn about their policies.)

•

What is the difference between a college and a university?

A college refers to a program that confers a bachelor's degree. All students of a college are undergraduates. Some colleges are part of a larger institution (university) and others are entities unto themselves, devoted to a particular discipline, including but not limited to engineering, business and arts and sciences.

A university is an educational institution that combines one or more colleges, often conferring graduate degrees including, but not limited to MD, DDS, MBA, JD and Ph.D. For example, the University of Pennsylvania is the umbrella name of a university that is comprised of several colleges including The College (Arts and Sciences), Wharton (the Business School) and the School of Engineering.

•

What is a community college?

A community college is a two-year school where students receive college credits. Some students attend community college if they do not have the necessary grades or test scores for a four-year college. Other students attend a community college to figure out what they want to do in life before spending a lot of money and later transferring to a four-year college. Additionally, students might opt to attend a community college if they are planning to go to school part-time and possibly working while attending school. Community colleges accept students of a wide academic and socio-economic range. Credits at a community college cost significantly less than they do at a four-year college.

• • •

Advanced Placement (AP) Courses/Exams

What is an AP Course?

Advanced Placement courses are considered to be college level courses in terms of scope and content. They are offered through high schools and in conjunction with the College Board and cover a wide range of subjects. AP courses should prepare students for an AP exams administered in May.

•

Should an AP Score of 3 be sent to colleges during the application process?

Yes. Although colleges typically offer advanced placement or grant college credit--or both--for AP scores of 4 or 5, a significant number of colleges will also recognize an AP score of 3.

•

Can one or more AP scores be withheld from colleges?

Yes. Students can withhold or even cancel one or more scores, but AP Services must receive the written request no later than June 15th. If your child decides to withhold a score, it can still be sent later if desired. However, cancelled scores are permanently deleted. For details, follow this link: apscore.collegeboard.org/scores/score-reporting.

•

How are AP scores sent to colleges?

Scores can be sent to colleges and viewed online through this website: www.apscore.org. If you have any questions, the number for students and parents to call is 1-888-Call4AP.

•

How important is it to take one or more AP courses in high school?

It depends on the tier of college or university for which your child is aiming. Typically, the most competitive colleges are more likely to accept students who have enrolled in additional AP courses. Thus, it makes sense for your child to enroll in as demanding a course load as possible throughout his/her high school years. However, AP courses are not for everyone, and some students might become either overwhelmed or stretched so thin that grades suffer as a result.

•

Is it better to do better in a regular course as opposed to doing less well in an AP course?

This question comes up often. The best answer is that your child should be in the class where he/she can be most successful. Colleges want students to challenge themselves in rigorous courses and do well. If your child is struggling in an AP course, he/she should discuss with the teacher whether the course is the right fit. For selective colleges, student applicants are taking an array of AP courses and will need to do well in them in order to be competitive.

• • •

Will colleges accept SAT or ACT scores listed on the high school transcript, or do they require original copies?

Colleges generally require original copies of standardized test results. Send original scores directly from the testing company. For the SAT and SAT Subject Tests, go to www.collegeboard.org, and for the ACT go to www.act.org. The Score Choice option allows students to submit SAT and ACT scores by test date, and SAT Subject Test by test. Colleges will either ask for all scores, or will accept the highest scores from whatever test dates your child submits, which is known as "superscoring."

If a college asks for all SAT or ACT test dates to be submitted and you're tempted to try and bypass that requirement, we urge you not to do so. Colleges can contact guidance counselors to inquire about whether or not a student took the SAT, SAT Subject Test or ACT on a particular test date. Don't try to circumvent the requirement because the consequence can result in the student being rejected. Colleges try to give students the benefit of the doubt, and if there's a legitimate reason why a particular set of scores was below expectation, the school counselor should be informed. For example, if someone in the family just had surgery, or there was a recent divorce, it would explain why a student's test scores were below par. When in doubt, either you or your child should talk with the guidance counselor, who can incorporate this relevant information in the school recommendation.

•

The high school transcript/GPA weighs AP and Honors courses. Will that help my child get into college?

Research has shown that high schools that weigh AP and/or Honors courses appear to offer students an advantage. That said, many colleges have their own internal system of recalculating all grades from secondary schools that weigh or don't weigh grade point averages in order to level the playing field. Some of these colleges omit freshman year grades when recalculating. Other colleges may use the high school profile for guidance. The school profile typically offers an overview of the community, while providing facts and figures, including standardized test data, graduation rates, student achievement, Advanced Placement courses offered and an overall academic synopsis.

•

Does senior year count for college admission?

Not only does it count, it can make the difference between being accepted or rejected. Most colleges will want to see your child's midyear grades, which typically include first and second quarter grades. Also, the high school transcript with senior year final grades will be sent to the college your son or daughter plans to attend. Any significant drop in grades can have serious consequences. Those consequences typically range from a written reprimand to putting the student on probation. In extreme cases, the college might even rescind a positive admissions decision. The bottom line is that colleges expect the final transcript sent by your child's high school to reflect grades comparable to past performance. It's never too early for your child to get serious about academic performance. It's important to recognize that colleges look at trends in your child's academic program from 9th to 12th grades.

If their scholastic "trajectory" is on an upswing, it demonstrates maturity and steady progress during a student's high school years. If there is a downward trend in a student's high school record, it's crucial that they reverse the trend and improve performance. If there were any personal/family issues that contributed to a downward trend, even for a single year, it's important to notify the school counselor about it. The counselor can address it in his/her letter of recommendation to the colleges.

•

My student took AP classes and got "B's," but a number of classmates took all regular classes and got "A's" and "A-'s." Will my child be at a disadvantage?

No. While colleges prefer AP classes with grades in the A range, they recognize that higher-level courses are much more rigorous than the traditional high school course. According to many college admissions officers, the degree of rigor in the courses a student has taken is a significant criterion in evaluating that individual for admission. Admission offices usually want to see students take the most challenging courses. However, if a student's grades fall below a B-, we suggest the child talk with the school counselor and the subject teacher. Dropping down to the high school level course, if one is offered, may be the right move. Also, many schools only allow a course to be dropped without penalty (meaning, it won't appear on the high school transcript) during a specified window of time. So when a student is choosing courses, it's important to know from the outset what the school policy is regarding dropping a course.

•

Does a GPA consist of only major subjects, or does it include all courses?

It all depends on the individual high school. Many high schools include all courses except physical education. We suggest you or your child discuss it with the school counselor.

•

What is Naviance? If my school uses it, how do we use it to figure out whether my child's GPA will make him/her eligible for specific schools?

Many schools use a college information system called Naviance which has information about how your child's GPA will relate to getting into schools because of the GPA they require. Naviance will give you National Data and School Specific Data. Pay most attention to School Specific Data, which will give GPA and SAT/ACT data about where your child's school's students got in based on this information.

• • •

How much does a student's 11th grade record contribute to a student's application?

Considered almost universally to be the most challenging of all the high school years, 11th grade is when students are not only responsible for taking challenging courses, but are simultaneously preparing for standardized tests and often juggling a more independent social life. Colleges recognize that the competing academic and social pressures make time and stress management, as well as honed study skills and a solid work ethic, all critical to success. So the junior year record provides colleges with the most recent full-year indicator of how a student will perform under stressful conditions.

This isn't meant to suggest that other high school years don't count. Colleges evaluate your child's entire secondary school transcript including academic trends, and, of course, all high school years do contribute to the GPA (and rank, if your high school ranks).

•

What do colleges look for in an applicant?

Colleges look for students who stand out. They want well-rounded individuals who have dynamic special talents or abilities. They're also looking for students who not only fit within the upper range of their high school's academic profile, but also those whose background and extracurricular activities indicate that they will be active and contributing members of their college community. It's less about the quantity of activities and more about the quality of leadership and passion for their extracurricular activities.

•

My child took honors courses in 8th grade. Do they count in the GPA?

The high school GPA may encompass honors and accelerated classes from 8th grade, and will certainly include all courses from 9th grade onward, possibly excluding physical education. A number of high schools also give credit for foreign language in 8th grade depending on either the state education policy or local school district regulations.

•

Should my child apply to a school even if the GPA and/ or standardized test scores are lower than a college's published score range?

Selecting a range of schools taking into account safety, target and reaches is the way to go. Students should apply to reach schools with the understanding that while they're long shots, some of them might be looking for something that stands out other than grades and standardized test scores.

•

How can my child stand out to a college?

The high school record, standardized test scores, college essays, recommendation letters and extracurricular activities, along with the college interview (whenever recommended or required), all provide a collective picture of your child as a student and as a person. Students should challenge themselves academically, do their best, prepare seriously for the SAT/ACT, and take on leadership roles in extracurricular activities organizations. Students should research each school, and show that they are a good fit throughout their applications. Have them do their own due diligence. Additionally, if your child has any talent(s), let the colleges know. If they have had any significant experiences, or, for example, made a difference either

44

in someone's life, or in the school or community, don't keep it a secret. If students don't toot their own horns, no one will hear the music.

Bottom line: This is the time for your child to self-advocate. Highlight achievements both inside and outside of the classroom and demonstrate the ways your child will add to each school's campus environment. In life, your child will need to be his/her own best advocate. This is the ideal time to start!

• • •

My child is a member of eight clubs but has never held a position of leadership in any. Is that a problem?

It's all about quality, not quantity. Being a valued member of one or more school organizations will work in your child's favor, but rising to one or more positions of leadership will enhance an application significantly. In other words, being a member of three or four clubs and having leadership roles is preferable to being a member of eight clubs and having no positions of leadership. In either case, when it comes to applying to colleges, your school counselor will be getting feedback from the faculty advisors of these clubs and can incorporate activities, contributions, commitment and dedication in their letter of recommendation.

•

Is community service critical to an application?

Whenever an individual offers services free of charge that benefit either the public or an institution, it's considered community service. It's often organized through one's high school, though other organizations in the community, such as religious institutions or charities may offer opportunities for service. Listing it on an application is not critical, but it's often helpful. Colleges generally like to see students engaged in their communities. It tells them something about character, and it suggests that the student is an active participant in the school community.

•

How does my child make his or her activities stand out to a college?

As previously stated, colleges typically view students who have been active participants in their high school community as likely to be equally active contributors to their college community. On your child's application, begin by listing the activities and leadership roles for which he or she has the greatest passion. Hopefully those are also the ones participated in the longest. Consider having club advisors submit a statement to your child's school counselor highlighting contributions made to the organization. If the club is directly associated with a selected college major, consider having the advisor submit the letter directly to the school (i.e. if your child is a long time member of the computer science club and is majoring in computers in college). The same holds true if the organization has been a showcase for any talent.

•

If a student doesn't have many extracurricular school activities, will that hurt their chances?

It might. Colleges want their students to be active members of the campus community, so they do look for applicants who are engaged in their high schools. Sometimes, students can't give as much time as they would like for extracurricular activities because of family responsibilities, a job, or because they are pursuing a special talent through private instruction. It's important to let the colleges know the situation, rather than leave them to make assumptions.

•

My son/daughter is not involved in any school activities because he/she plays a musical instrument for several hours every afternoon. How can we let colleges know about this?

Give them as much information as possible about your child's music and private instruction. Consider having the music teacher submit either a supplemental letter of recommendation to colleges about your child's talent or comments to your guidance counselor that can be incorporated into the school recommendation.

• • •

My child plays on a sports team. Will that help with admissions?

That depends on a number of factors. For the committed athlete who has been playing competitively throughout many school years, the answer is an unequivocal "yes." If that athlete is also a gifted player, the advantages are obvious. Conversely, if your child joins a team during junior or senior year, the impact on college applications will likely be minimal.

•

But what about all those students in-between?

What colleges look for in terms of sports participation is commitment, ability, leadership, good sportsmanship and a willingness to get involved in the life of the school. So if your child's involvement on a sports team would demonstrate one or more of these traits in a positive light, then yes, this aspect of school life would be an advantage in applying to college.

•

What role, if any, does my child's coach play in the admissions process?

Your child's coach can guide your child by helping determine if a Division I, II or III college is the best fit. Furthermore, while it's your child's responsibility to reach out to college coaches, the high school coach can be an effective liaison between your child and the college coaches.

•

Should my child's coach and school counselor be in regular contact?

Regular contact isn't necessary. However, your counselor needs to get a feedback form from the coach, highlighting the child's strengths and abilities in the sport. This information will ultimately be incorporated into the college recommendation. High school coaches are also good people to contact as motivators if you sense your child is starting to fade academically at any point, especially in the senior year.

•

Will my child's coach contact the college coaches?

If your child is talented, demonstrates leadership abilities, and the coach is supportive, then he will likely reach out to his college level counterparts. Additionally, if your child goes to the Athletics Section of any college website, he/she should be able to get the coach's email and send him/her an introductory email about their desire to play on the team. That said, your child should continue to work together with the high school coach on everything involved in this process.

•

Is there anything else that is important to know?

Yes, and this is very important. If your child is applying to Division I and/or Division II schools, he/she must register with the NCAA Eligibility Center in the junior year. This is not necessary for Division III schools. Here are the steps to take:

a. Go to http://www.ncaa.org

b. Click Student- Athletes at the top of page.

c. You will be able to access the "Guide to College Bound Student Athlete" which has all the information you need to know.

d. Under the same heading go to NCAA Eligibility Center. Enter as a Student Athlete.

e. Click on "Resources" at the top of the page and go to "Forms." You child must print the Transcript Release Form and give it to his/her counselor so their transcript can be sent. At "Resources" you can also have another opportunity to access the "Guide to College Bound Student Athlete."

f. If you want to find out which schools offer which sports, click on "Sports" at the top of the page and flip through pages 2-5.

g. It's most important that your child register for an account at the top right hand corner and complete all the necessary questions and get an ID number.

h. All this information should be shared with both your child's counselor and coach.

Registration is very, very important because it will determine if your child has the academic profile to play Division I or II sports based on their GPA in combination with SAT/ACT scores. When students register, they will need to download a Transcript Release Form found at the website and give it to their counselor so he/she can forward your child's high school transcript and continue sending updated transcripts through the end of senior year. This Eligibility Center/Clearinghouse will list all of your child's high school's course offerings and in addition to the transcript, will need your son's/daughter's SAT/ACT scores in order to evaluate and clear a student to be eligible to play. At the website you will be able to access a guide, "The Prospective Student Athlete" and read all about the rules, including the recruiting and scholarship rules for athletes.

•

Shouldn't my child be mostly focused on how well he/she is going to do in college?

Yes. In the term "Student-Athlete," your child should realize that he/she is a student first, and must choose an appropriate school where they can be a successful student and balance both academics and athletics. Your son/daughter must meet with college coaches to see what kind of tutoring and support services are given to student athletes, and at the end of the day, he/she must choose a college which is the best fit and where they can be most successful. Many student athletes are recruited by very selective schools because they are so athletically talented, but the academics of the schools are way too difficult.

• • •

The Performing and Visual Arts Student

My child is interested in studying one of the performing or visual arts (art, drama, musical theatre, music performance or dance). Where do we start?

A good starting place is NACAC's (National Association of College Admissions Counselors) website. In addition to "Tips for the Performing and Visual Arts Student," there is information about Performing Arts College Fairs around the country, where schools with these programs will be represented. You and your child will be able to speak with representatives at colleges which offer these specific programs and pick up informational brochures.

    a. Go to http://nacacnet.org

    b. Click "College Fairs" at the top of the page.

    c. Click "Performing and Visual Arts Fair Schedule".

    d. On the right side of the page you will see fair schedules, how to get started and tips you and your child need to know.

•

How will this route affect the college process?

In addition to the application for admission, there will be auditions (for music, dance and theatre students) as well as portfolio requirements for art students. These requirements and procedures for fulfilling them will be listed on the college website.

•

Does this involve more deadlines, supplements, and layers to the whole process?

Yes, and sometimes it can get very demanding. You child will need to arrange for pre-auditions/auditions, portfolio review, etc., and this can also involve an additional section of the application.

•

How will my child know how to submit supplemental materials such as an art portfolio or YouTube video of acting, singing, dancing, etc.?

When your child fills out the application and checks off his/her desired program, there will be information about this process. Many colleges ask students to use "Slideroom" to submit these materials.

•

What is Slideroom?

Slideroom (http://www.slideroom.com) partners with the Common Application so students can send media within the application process. When your child applies to a particular school for an arts program, he/she may be directed to Slideroom to submit the required materials.

•

I want my child to have other opportunities outside of the arts just in case he/she doesn't become that famous actor, musician, dancer or singer he/she hopes to be. How can we make sure that other schools are chosen that have other opportunities?

Some schools are totally focused on a specific arts area: music conservatories and art schools have few opportunities for study outside of the student's chosen area of focus. Other schools and universities may have a School of Music or a School of Visual Arts within the larger university setting. Attending such a school will give a student more opportunities to study other disciplines, while also maintaining a study of the arts.

•

I heard that if a student is very talented but is not such a great student, their talent will get them into college. Is this true?

At many schools, students are evaluated for talent, but also evaluated on their academic performance. Thus, both are important factors in the admissions process. Conservatories and Art Schools of course are looking mainly at talent. Some schools will allow students to submit proof of their creative talent, though they may not want to major in that area, and schools will use this additional information in the admissions process which can help students.

•

My child works with a private music teacher, gets private art or singing lessons and/or is involved in his/ her school's drama program, art program, etc. Should we bounce things off these instructors and faculty advisors?

Absolutely, bring everybody into the discussion to assess your child's ability in an effort to move forward realistically. These people can be great resources in addition to the school counselor.

•

Will my child need a separate resume which highlights all experiences in his/her chosen area of interest?

It is a good idea to develop this type of resume to send with application materials. Upload it as a supplement to your child's application and bring it to interviews, auditions and portfolio reviews.

• • •

How important are summer activities to colleges?

Summer activities provide a window to colleges about how your child spends his/her free time. Is your child reading, traveling, doing community service, taking an enrichment or college-level course, or working? Or does summer mean loafing around, doing nothing but sleeping late, going on Facebook, hanging out, tweeting, playing video games and texting? There is a difference.

•

My child did nothing last summer except sleep late and have fun. Will that hurt an application?

If a college likes your child's overall credentials, then summer activities won't likely be a factor in admission. However, when it comes to reach schools, every little bit of insurance matters. For example, imagine there are 10 remaining slots to be filled in a freshman class, and there are 20 applicants. Assuming the applicants all have similar credentials, but 10 had very productive summers and the others lounged around, guess who would have the edge?

•

How can I find out about different summer opportunities for my child?

Check with your child's school counselor and check your child's school' website at the guidance section. Guidance offices receive tons of mail about summer programs and may inform students and parents in many different ways. There is nothing wrong with getting a summer job to save money for college and to develop responsible working skills. Colleges truly respect this choice. If your child is interested in a specific college, check the college's website for "Summer Programs for

High School Students." Spending a couple of weeks on a college campus, one that interests you, is a great way to experience the campus, the classes and the college environment. Be aware that some of these programs are expensive, and applications need to be in as early as January of senior year.

•

My child likes to travel. Will that help an application?

It might. If it involves occasional traveling with family or friends, that likely won't make a difference. However, if the travel is purposeful or enriching, it could certainly make for a more interesting and possibly stronger application. For example, if your child traveled to a third world country and helped build homes or plant crops, that would be a plus. Or perhaps the travel could be tied in to an academic strength or career dream. If your child took college level courses in another country, that, too, would be advantageous.

•

Should we ask for a letter from an employer, camp counselor or supervisor to give to the school counselor?

Any positive learning experience your child has should conclude with a request for a recommendation letter at the end of the summer. The mentor (camp counselor, teacher, professor, coach, supervisor, etc.) should write a recommendation and send it to your child's school counselor. This will provide the counselor with another useful perspective, broadening and enriching the college letter of recommendation.

•

What is one major activity that all rising seniors must do in the summer before senior year?

The Common Application, used by most colleges, goes live on August 1. Your child should register for an account on August 1 and work on completing the Common Application before school officially begins. Many school's supplements may not be available until the fall, but your child can complete the core of the application. Essay questions are usually released in March.

• • •

Does having a college interview help one's chances of being accepted?

While some college interviews will become a part of the admissions process, they usually only highlight things that are already listed in the application. In the interview, colleges hope to learn more about the kind of student your child would be in their classes, living in their dorms and participating in their campus life. If an interview is neither required nor recommended, or if it's a group interview, then it's not going to be a factor in the admissions decision.

If there were any unusual circumstances during high school, such as a divorce or death of someone in your family and it had an impact on their grades, an informal interview might be helpful in conveying the specific circumstances. Having a college interview can certainly help a student's chances if it's required or recommended. If that's the case, we suggest that your child prepare for the interview in advance either with his/her guidance counselor or with a private college advisor.

•

What should my child wear to a college interview, and what is the best way to prepare?

The college interview can help bring an application to life, but, you should remember that it won't weigh too heavily on the admission decision. That being said, we would suggest dressing casually and neat. It's not a black tie event, but students should wear appropriate attire.

To prepare, consider doing some role-playing situations with the guidance counselor; practice does help. Also your child should prepare one or two thoughtful questions to ask your interviewer. Bring a student copy of their high school transcript in case the interviewer would like to refer to it; this shows good foresight on their part. Your child may also bring a resume. Be certain cell phones are turned off and kept out of sight.

If, during the interview, your child is asked a question that is totally unexpected, they should not attempt to rush a response. It's okay to pause, or say, "Let me think about that for a moment." Another good way to handle a difficult question is to rephrase the interviewer's question and ask if the question was correctly understood. It may also prompt the interviewer to give your child a bit more of a lead about what they're looking for.

•

What sort of questions should a student prepare to ask at the interview?

Students should prepare a few questions that will demonstrate serious research about this college. Thus, avoid questions that could have been easily answered by browsing the college's website or in the literature the student read regarding academics, campus life, clubs and community service opportunities. Students can ask about safety on campus, about the college's retention rate, or even about career advisement for students entering senior year. Questions should not suggest that your student knows very little about the college. For example, don't ask if the college offers a major in Biology, or if the dorms are co-ed. Your child might even want to ask them to talk their favorite feature/ aspect/ opportunity of campus life.

•

Is it appropriate to use a college interview as an opportunity to explain some special circumstances that affected a student's high school performance?

Yes, it's appropriate to use this opportunity to discuss any potential red flags on a student's transcript, but be honest. Your child doesn't want a lie to come back and bite. For example, if asked why grades slipped freshman year, it's okay to tell the interviewer that about a divorce or an illness. If, on the other hand, the real reason grades were lower than they should have been was because of friends, relationships, or some other distractions, students might want to acknowledge the missteps but say that they have done a lot of growing up and now have their priorities in order, as demonstrated in recent academic reports. They should always think beforehand about any possible negatives, and discuss them with school counselors and family members first. The counselor's letter of recommendation will complement your child's honest comments in a way that will be beneficial.

•

What are the magic words that will make my child the one they choose?

There are no magic words, unfortunately. But there are some very powerful ways that your child can increase their chances to stand out. Know the college well enough to prepare intelligent questions to ask during the interview. Suggest going into the interview with a confident mindset and greeting the interviewer with a smile, making direct eye contact and offering a solid handshake. During the interview, maintain good eye contact and thank the interviewer for her time and attention. Then, follow up by sending a thank you note. Attention to these small but important details makes a strong and favorable impression. Everything your child says and does tells the college something. This can help differentiate applicants who may be similar in a number of other categories.

•

Is an alumni interview as good as an on-campus interview?

It's fine, but don't use it as a substitute for visiting the college, if circumstances permit. Colleges generally keep track of who comes to visit through camps tours and on-site interviews.

If your child applies somewhere Early Action, it can be advantageous to visit that college in advance. However, if your child applies Early Decision, it is imperative that he/she visits that college before making a binding commitment. If making it to the college in person is not possible, try to insure your child makes an effort to demonstrate interest beyond passively looking at the college website or quietly sitting in the back of high school information sessions.

•

A representative from a college my child is interested in attending is coming to the high school to talk with students. Is there anything my child should do or ask?

During the meeting, your child should listen intently (no distractions), get any handouts or brochures offered and take notes. After the conference, suggest that your child ask for the representative's business card, which will have contact information on it, and ask for permission to call or email with any further questions. Be sure that you remind your child to say thank you and shake hands before leaving and send a follow-up email soon after the session, letting the representative know some specific things about the college that were particularly attractive or intriguing about the school.

•

My child was not asked to have an alumni interview. Does that mean he/she is not being considered for admission?

No. Sometimes colleges just don't have the time or resources to meet with everyone. Just make sure your child keeps working hard! It will not affect your child's application in any way.

•

My child had an interview (either on-campus or alumni) and it only lasted 20 minutes. Does that mean the college is no longer interested?

Not at all. Interviews can range in time from 15 minutes to over an hour.

•

Should a thank you email be sent after attending interviews and information sessions?

It's highly recommended to do so. A thank you note demonstrates maturity and will further differentiate your child from other applicants. It will take five minutes to send a message of appreciation to the interviewer. It can't hurt, it just might help, and it's simply the right thing to do.

•

When should students sign up to visit college campuses?

The best time is in the spring of junior year. That's when the regular student body is present, and students will get to see campus life firsthand. While it's more convenient to visit during the summer, your child won't get a feel for the social atmosphere of the campus in full swing. If they are too busy during the school year, visit colleges in late August or early September and then re-visit the one or two that they were top choices later on.

•

What else should students do besides take an organized tour?

Talk to students on campus, check out the college bookstore, visit the admissions office and eat in the students' dining hall. If the college either requires or recommends an interview, schedule it in advance for that same day. Also, get a copy of the school's newspaper and go to open houses. Your child should bring a pen and paper and take notes about impressions, both positive and negative, because once you start visiting colleges, remembering details does become hazy. If your child is interested in a particular academic area, he/she should try to make an appointment to speak with someone in the department. After the visit, if your child likes the school, he/she should sign up to be on the school's mailing/email list. This can be done on the college website.

•

Can my child sit in on classes? Stay overnight?

Your child can stay overnight with a friend, and, if any professor permits it, attend one or more classes (this should be arranged in advance). Ask the high school counselor if there's a contact list of any recent graduates who are willing to be available to talk with, meet with, or offer housing to prospective students.

•

Should my child arrange to speak with anyone in particular on campus?

If your child met anyone from the college who previously visited their high school, all efforts should be made to see them. Email the college representative in advance to be sure they'll be available on the day of your child's visit. If they're out of town when you visit the campus, see if your child can meet with someone else in the admissions office. We also encourage striking up informal conversations with students on campus, particularly students in the cafeteria, in the library, or in the halls of classrooms specific to your child's interests (i.e. in the labs if they love science), gleaning valuable student perspectives about each college.

• • •

What is the college essay used for?

It gives the colleges a chance to learn more about your child's personality, writing style, priorities and beliefs. It's important that a family member and an English teacher review what your child writes and offer recommendations. Your school counselor can also be a reader. A well-written, insightful essay can make a huge difference.

•

My child is having trouble selecting a topic for the personal statement. Any suggestions?

Begin by looking through the activities list, community service or paid work efforts and other life altering or meaningful experiences. Try to find a defining incident, significant accomplishment, "Aha" moment or an outstanding aspect of a particular "story" that can be captured in an engaging essay. The essay gives the admissions officers a memorable perspective of applicants and helps them stand out among hundreds of other students.

•

Who should my child ask to proofread their college essay?

Colleges expect students to submit a polished essay. Therefore, it is valuable to have some objective readers take a look at the essay before submitting it. Students can reach out to mentors such as a guidance counselor or English teacher. Parents can also help proofread and give suggestions.

•

How important is the college essay?

The college essay is one of the most important determining factors in the admission process. It brings a student's voice to the application, creating the best opportunity to share views and experiences with admissions officers. It is essential that your child write self-reflective essays that both provoke thought and engage interest. It's also important to respect the suggested word counts and strive to be on-point and succinct.

•

Are there any off-limits topics?

Nothing is off-limits, but common sense should dictate your child's choice of subject matter. If your child is thinking about sharing any controversial topic, run it by both family members and the guidance counselor in advance.

•

Can students exceed the word limit?

Admission offices like applicants that don't go over the word count. Online applications such as the Common Application typically don't allow that; the essay will be cut off once the word limit has been reached. Much more than 25 words beyond what's expected is more likely to hurt rather than help, though many schools do not mind as long as the additional text is within reason and directly helpful in portraying the applicant. On the Common Application, there is a minimum requirement of 250 words and a maximum limit of 650 words for the personal statement.

Supplemental essays vary in length by school and topic, so endeavor to stay within the limits while using as much real estate as possible to make the application stand out.

• • •

How many letters of recommendation do students need from teachers?

Colleges typically require the school counselor letter of recommendation as well as the School Report along with either one or two teacher recommendations. Your child can submit an additional letter or two, but they should come from individuals with a different perspective, such as a coach, school principal or other significant person in a student's life. Sending more recommendations does not increase your chance of being admitted, so most admission officers prefer you to stick within their recommendation guidelines.

•

Which teachers should students ask to write college recommendation?

Your child should try to elicit recommendations from the teachers of their strongest subjects that reflect his or her choice of college major (if already known). For example, if your child wants to major in journalism, consider asking an 11th grade English teacher; an accounting major might ask an 11th grade math teacher. In general, colleges want recommendations to be written by 11th grade teachers, preferably a Math/Science teacher and an English/Social Studies/Foreign Language teacher. Sometimes a letter of recommendation from a teacher of a class in which your child did not do as well can be the best letter. If the student struggled, worked really hard and met with the teacher continuously for extra help, the teacher can elaborate on the student's strong work ethic in a very challenging class. Colleges will see that the student is very persevering and that he/she will use all the resources of the college to succeed.

We agree with the current trend at colleges such as Yale

and SUNY Binghamton that recommend students ask for reference letters from teachers who know them best, with whom there has been a sustained relationship and who can reflect on your child's work ethic. While 11th grade teachers are excellent candidates to write recommendation letters, they should not exclude a 10th grade teacher who may know your child better, and who has maintained a relationship through extracurricular activities or community service.

•

My guidance counselor really doesn't know my child well. Will that hurt his/her chances?

Probably not. Your child's guidance counselor uses a number of resources to write letters of recommendation, including a student's guidance records, high school transcript, standardized test scores and feedback from teachers they've had during their high school years, including anecdotes that your child might be encouraged to gather. Parents and students can give counselors insight about the student's greatest strengths, most outstanding accomplishments and any circumstances that may have impacted their educational or personal experience. Keep in mind as well that it's never too late for your child to make an appointment with his/her guidance counselor to provide any new information, share any concerns, or just get to know them better.

•

Should students waive their right to read teacher recommendations?

Definitely. Waiving the right to read teacher recommendations signals to colleges that whatever teachers and counselors write about your child will be an honest evaluation of high school performance. Not signing the waiver is a red flag, and typically results in a reference letter that is less than candid, and colleges would find suspect. Signing the waiver significantly increases the value of the submitted recommendations, which, in turn, enhances your child's credentials.

•

I'm worried that a teacher might write a bad recommendation about my child.

Teachers are not looking to hurt students. If your child approaches a teacher about a letter of recommendation for college and receives an enthusiastic "yes," trust the educator. Writing a recommendation takes a lot of time and effort, so professionals aren't going to waste their time writing a letter that's going to hurt your son or daughter. At the same time, if your child asks an instructor to write a letter, and he or she makes an excuse such as, "I'm too busy now" or questions if they're the best person to ask, your child should take the hint and ask another teacher.

•

Our priest/rabbi has known my child for many years. Should a religious figure be asked to write a recommendation? Should we send in supplemental letters of recommendation from a coach or employer?

Supplemental letters that share useful information about your child are always welcome, as long as an applicant doesn't go overboard and send too many. Your child can either have these individuals submit letters directly to the colleges, or ask them to send their comments to a guidance counselor, who can incorporate that information into the school recommendation. Generally, having your child's counselor include such comments in a school recommendation works best.

• • •

FEEDBACK FORMS TO SHARE WITH THE GUIDANCE COUNSELOR

What is a "feedback form"?

A feedback form provides the school counselor with relevant and useful information about your child from people who know your child very well, based on significant interactions, whether in the classroom, on the athletic field, or through an important extracurricular activity in or out of school. This form, often called "an anecdotal," is used solely by your child's school counselor and is never sent to any colleges. However, it can provide invaluable insights to your child's guidance counselor when preparing their letter of recommendation. These feedback forms differ from the official letters of recommendation that teachers send directly to colleges either by mail or electronically through software programs such as Naviance.

•

Why is a feedback form helpful?

The school counselor typically knows your child through their guidance file, group sessions and individual counselor meetings. The feedback forms provide the counselor with the voices of others who know your child from different perspectives, permitting a much more enriched perception of your child, and allowing the counselor to write a more thorough and nuanced recommendation. Remembering to distribute these forms is an important and strategic step that will be clearly beneficial.

•

How do I know that teachers will only write positive things about my child?

You don't, which is why your child should choose carefully (i.e. Which teachers know me best? Where have I had the most positive experiences?). Even if a teacher submits a less than glowing form, the counselor is under no obligation to include that in the letter of recommendation.

Your child's counselor will review all of the gathered information and ultimately, will use discretion to best represent your child to the colleges.

•

What about feedback from someone other than my child's teachers?

The feedback forms can be given to anyone who knows your child well. A coach, extracurricular activities advisor, a religious figure in your church, synagogue or mosque, employer, or a family member—any of these could offer a unique perspective of your child that would add an important dimension about the student.

•

Should anyone in our family submit a feedback form for my child?

Absolutely. You know your child better than anyone, and can address what you view as your child's greatest achievements, list adjectives, highlight strengths, describe any circumstances that may have impacted your child's performance or well-being in school, and anything else you feel is pertinent. We also recommend that your child complete a self-reflection feedback form, answering some or all of the same questions asked of you. In addition, your child can highlight any particular talents and significant school or community activities, sharing why these aspects hold such importance. This is your child's chance to shine. The more information the school counselor has about your child, the better.

•

My child's school doesn't offer feedback forms. What should we do?

Even if your child's school does not offer feedback forms, there's no reason why you and your child cannot go ahead and submit your own written comments to share with the school counselor. Additionally, have your child ask favorite teachers to write a short blurb and submit it to the counselor.

•

My child has a job. Should he give a feedback form to an employer?

If your child has worked at a particular job on a regular basis and is close with their supervisor, then a feedback form from that individual would be helpful to show work ethic and job performance. Employers can either give the student's counselor a feedback form or write a blurb. Either way, check with the college to find out whether the recommendation should be mailed to your child's school counselor or to the college directly.

•

Should my child give a feedback form to a teacher from this current senior year?

It depends. If your child is applying to one or more colleges Early Decision (ED) or Early Action (EA), there's little time for a teacher to truly get to know the student. The school counselor should not be held up on sending a recommendation out while waiting for the teacher's feedback form. However, if your child previously had the same teacher and had a good experience, then it could be considered. Also, if your child is not applying either ED or EA, then there may be enough time for a current teacher to develop a constructive relationship with your child in order to write a helpful recommendation.

• • •

Do we need to worry about a college searching for students on social media networks?

In a word—absolutely! Admission officers do not always look for students on social media networks, but that doesn't mean students shouldn't present themselves well online. Online scrutiny of college applicants is growing, and a student's digital footprint can play a significant role in the admissions process.

What your child shares online may be viewable by many—those "privacy settings" have to be closely monitored! So assume all these people may be looking online to gather additional information about your child's character and activities: college admissions officers, scholarship coordinators, financial aid officers, athletic recruiters, teachers who are writing recommendations, potential employers for internships and jobs and assorted other organizations.

•

What precautions should my child take to make sure the online image he/she has on all social media accounts (including Facebook, Google, YouTube, Pinterest, Twitter, Tumblr, Vine, Instagram and Foursquare) will be as appropriate and free of potentially damaging material as possible?

Your child should review ALL social media profiles, as there may be some that are linked to one another. A privacy setting enables the user to determine who is allowed to view all postings, photos, tags and "likes." Regularly monitoring these settings enables the student to remain in control of what others can see. Remind your child to be certain that there are no inappropriate posts or photos dating back to when an account was opened with each particular social media site.

Photos of the student drinking alcohol (or any illegal activity), being in the company of others who are engaging in these activities, using rude or profane language or gestures, or participating in any sexual or sexually suggestive activities are the sort of incriminating posts and pictures your child should delete immediately.

Encourage your child to check for any "tags" and pages that may have been "liked" that could be compromising or embarrassing. This may seem less obvious, but providing private contact information such as a phone number or address, demonstrates poor judgment, and even the username and handles that your child chooses to use are revelatory to an astute observer. So a simple, direct username and a professional profile with a dignified photo will make an appropriate statement. At the same time, your child should be proactive in cultivating a positive profile on social media sites. The groups students join, the pages they "like" and the posts they make can provide a view into interesting and unexpected dimensions of students' lives.

Finally, admissions officers (and others like potential employers) are technology-savvy and well aware that students maintain two Facebook accounts. In short, keep them wholesome!

• • •

Senior Year:
The Fall Semester

How important is the fall semester? Why does it count as heavily as the junior year?

Colleges place significance on the junior year and the fall semester of senior year. The fall semester of senior year provides colleges with the most up-to-date information about your child's scholastic performance in what is typically the most academically rigorous curriculum of a high school career. As juniors balance an increasingly demanding course load with extracurricular activities while also devoting hours to prepare for and then take multiple standardized tests, colleges believe students are learning to handle the level of pressure that undergraduate studies will demand. Those students who continue to excel during these school years impress colleges as good candidates for admission.

•

What if my child doesn't do well the first quarter of senior year?

The student must identify the source of difficulty and rectify the situation as quickly as possible. If your child is considering dropping a course, look up the deadline to ensure the course won't appear as "withdrawn" on the transcript. If there's any doubt, speak to the school counselor as soon as possible.

•

Should we send first quarter grades to colleges that my child applied to Early Decision or Early Action?

Yes, especially if they represent a steadiness of grades in prior years and certainly if they demonstrate a positive upturn in grades. In either case, your child may want to talk with his/her guidance counselor before making a final decision.

•

My child did very well in four of his five academic courses. Should we still send first quarter grades?

This depends on which course was weakest, the grade and previous grades in that subject. In general, as long as grades, especially in academic subjects, are at least as good as or better than in prior years, we recommend sending them.

• • •

Do students get accepted from the waitlist?

The waitlist is designed to inform applicants that colleges are serious about them; otherwise the student would have received a letter of denial. When colleges hear back from admitted students regarding the acceptance of their offers, spots will open up on the waitlist. At that point, colleges will contact those students that they placed on the waitlist, offering some of them admission.

•

Is there anything a student can do to improve the chance of being accepted from the waitlist?

Certainly. In the body of an email (not as an attachment) to the Office of Undergraduate Admissions, copying the local recruiter, the student must state the tidbits of information that are relevant since submission of the original application:

1. Acknowledge that the student has been deferred or waitlisted.

2. State that the school remains the student's first choice (colleges love to admit students when they know it is the student's dream school).

3. Promise to attend if admitted (if this REALLY is the case).

4. Update any information (i.e. honors, awards, contests, competitions, scholarships, publications, jobs, community service endeavors, tutoring, new athletic, musical or artistic developments, club activities, visits to the college campus, meeting with professors, securing a summer job, commencement speaker, etc.).

5. Send first and second semester grades. Have your child state that he or she has remained steadfast and academically focused while juggling a more demanding course load, remaining an active participant in both the school and community and preparing for standardized tests.

6. Send significant standardized test score increases.

7. Reiterate the student's hope that this new information will help convince the school to admit him or her to the Class of_____.

8. Give an in-depth focus on the most impressive new qualification in detail, emphasizing how this achievement will help make a positive contribution to the college. Do some additional research on the college and discuss how the student envisions life on campus. Be specific about the courses, professors and clubs that the student is most excited about.

9. Request that this email update be included in the student's admission application folder. State that the student is hoping for good news.

10. Remember to include full name, address, cell number, email address, ID number and date of birth.

11. Follow up the email with a phone call to ensure that the Admissions Office has received the email, and that it has been added to the student's application folder.

12. Even if your child has already visited the school, if it is among the student's first choice schools, visit again. Putting a face to a name and an application demonstrates genuine interest. While there, your child can then restate goals and enthusiastically discuss the contributions to the campus he or she is

eager to make. Arrange another visit to the school, attend classes and meet with a professor in an area of interest. In a follow-up email, be sure to mention the specific details of your additional visit along with sincere thanks.

•

Do we have to put a deposit at another school while we wait to see if my child gets accepted from the waitlist?

Because there is no guarantee that the student will ultimately be accepted, and may even find out just prior to the start of classes in the fall, it is critical that the student seriously consider another school. Most schools require a commitment by May 1, along with a deposit. In fact, some schools require a dorm commitment prior to May 1. Therefore you must place a deposit at another school.

•

My child was admitted from the waitlist. Can I get my deposit back from the other colleges?

Not likely, since most deposits are nonrefundable. However, there's no harm in calling the Office of Undergraduate Admissions to inquire.

• • •

What is an IB Diploma Programme?

The IB Diploma Programme is an academically challenging, intercultural course of study intended to prepare students not only for college but also for life after their college career. It has a holistic approach, addressing the intellectual, social, emotional, ethical and physical aspects of the student's life in preparation for higher education and "real world" situations.

•

Can it help my child's chances for getting into college?

The IB offers a rigorous program of study that is considered comparable to Advanced Placement coursework among the more than 2,000 colleges and universities worldwide that recognize the diploma. Just like Advanced Placement courses, it's important to maintain strong grades.

Achieving excellent grades in this program--as in any program--will be advantageous to your child when applying to colleges. If your child is an IB candidate, it is best to contact colleges to confirm the university's policy on students with IB diplomas, and whether or not the diploma is recognized.

•

Does a student with an IB Program look better than a student enrolled in AP courses?

It depends. Students who plan to earn a traditional high school diploma can choose the number and type of Advanced Placement courses in which they wish to enroll. Students in IB programs have a mandatory set of core requirements including community service, an extended 4000-word essay/research paper and six interdisciplinary courses. The interdisciplinary curriculum, which provides the student with a broad depth of knowledge, comes from the following disciplines: Studies in Language and Literature, Language Acquisition, Individuals and Societies, Sciences, Mathematics and the Arts.

Another core requirement is the TOK (Theory of Knowledge) and additional information can be found at www.ibo.org/ diploma/curriculum/core/knowledge.

In addition, IB candidates must pass IB exams just as students in the AP program will take AP exams. Visit www.ibo.org/ diploma and www.ibo.org/diploma/curriculum for additional information.

•

Do all colleges accept an IB degree?

While over 2,000 institutions worldwide recognize the IB Diploma Programme, not every university will accept IB credits. Thus, we recommend contacting any college your child is thinking of applying to in advance to check out policies regarding IB diplomas. For a link to colleges and universities in the United States that recognize the IB Diploma as of the time of this publication, check www.ibo.org/country/US/index.cfm for further information.

•

Do colleges prefer an IB diploma or a regular high school diploma?

Colleges and universities that recognize the IB Diploma will view it as comparable to a diploma featuring a traditional AP program. However, since the IB degree requires a mandated curriculum, and the AP program does not, students in the traditional high school diploma program must choose to enroll in the more and most rigorous academic courses available. In addition, they need to participate in extracurricular activities that facilitate their emotional and social well-being, and they must be contributing members of their high school community.

• • •

If my child has either an IEP or Section 504 Plan, should it be shared with colleges?

You should share this information if your child is going to need accommodations or services related to the disability. The timing will depend on the particular college your child is applying to and the nature of the support you are seeking. Colleges with comprehensive or structured programs often have a separate admissions process and will want to see documentation of your child's disability early. If it's just basic services such as testing accommodations that are needed, there's no need to disclose the disability until after admission. Be sure to research the individual schools and programs and follow their instructions.

•

Will my child's learning differences affect admission?

No. Your child is protected under Section 504 of the Rehabilitation Act of 1973 and the Americans with Disabilities Act (ADA). These are federal civil rights statutes that prohibit discrimination against otherwise qualified individuals—people who meet the usual academic standards required for admission to a particular college. These laws mean that colleges may not place quotas on the number of students with disabilities they accept, and they may not require students to disclose their disabilities. They also require colleges to provide reasonable accommodations. (See question "Do all colleges provide services for students with disabilities?")

Sometimes, it can actually be beneficial to share information about your child's disability because it may help explain certain aspects of a transcript (e.g. no foreign language) and demonstrate a determination and ability to overcome obstacles.

•

Does my child first have to be accepted into the university in order to be accepted into a comprehensive or structured program?

It depends on the school. Each college sets its own admissions standards. Generally, your child will need to be admitted to the college before being considered for comprehensive services. However, there are instances where the regular admissions office and the support program make admissions decisions in consultation with one another.

•

Do all colleges provide services for students with disabilities?

Section 504 and the ADA require all colleges to provide reasonable accommodations in the areas of program, instruction and testing to ensure that they do not discriminate against the student with a disability. Requested accommodations must be directly linked to the student's disability through documentation. Colleges must provide access; they do not have to ensure success. Colleges have considerable latitude in what is reasonable. Examples of accommodations that are provided by most colleges include: reduced course load, audio books, note-takers and extended time on tests. It is important to gather as much information as possible about each school under consideration to be sure your child's specific needs will be met.

•

What are the differences between colleges that offer comprehensive programs and those that offer only basic services?

College support programs run the gamut. Virtually

all colleges offer at least basic services, such as testing accommodations and generic supports such as writing centers and peer tutoring. In colleges with basic services, the contact person wears many hats and may not have any specialized training. Generally, the student discloses his or her disability upon admission, not before. An increasing number of colleges have begun to offer comprehensive programs, which provide significantly more support. Individual tutorial assistance with specialists, frequent monitoring of student progress, special advisement and early registration are some of the enhanced services supervised by a full-time coordinator with expertise in learning disabilities and ADHD. Comprehensive programs typically have a separate application process and often carry a substantial additional cost. Students are advised to apply early because there may be limited slots.

•

What type of documentation of my child's disability is required?

Schools vary widely in how they handle the application process for students with special needs. Check the college's website by searching for "Disability Services." Many schools will outline specific documentation which is required. Schools with comprehensive programs usually require a separate application and essay, and often a letter of recommendation from your child's resource room teacher. At the minimum, colleges will want to see the most recent IEP or 504 Plan and documentation of disability in the form of a psycho-educational evaluation. Students with ADHD may be asked for a diagnostic statement from a medical professional. Before your child submits a regular application, find out exactly what documentation is required by each school. Also, ask to whom it should be mailed, and when. Your child's guidance counselor and resource room teacher will be able to help fulfill all documentation requirements.

•

How do we know which kind of program my child will need?

In considering what kind of program your child will need in college, think about the supports utilized during the last two years of high school. If your child is still dependent on direct, regular academic assistance, or receives some instruction in special education classes, it is a safe bet that a comprehensive program in college will be necessary. If your child is independent of nearly all supports by the end of high school, then the more basic services at a college will probably suffice. Another factor to weigh is how academically challenging the college itself is – the more competitive the school, the more help your child will likely require to be successful. If you're looking at schools with comprehensive programs, meeting with representatives of these programs is just as important as any other component of the college visits. In fact, if your child will need any level of services, you should include a visit to the Disabilities Office when visiting a school. Call ahead to make an appointment.

•

Should one of the letters of recommendation for college come from my child's resource room teacher?

If your child is applying to colleges with comprehensive programs, it makes sense to have a resource room teacher write a letter, especially if that teacher has come to know your child well and the two share a good relationship. If your child is only in need of basic services, then the resource room teacher could provide an extra reference letter or offer feedback to the school counselor to include in the college letter of recommendation. In either case, a letter from a resource room teacher should supplement, not replace, letters from mainstream classroom teachers.

•

A disability prevented my child from taking a foreign language. Will that hurt chances for admission?

Again, the answer is, "It depends." Some colleges require students to have taken at least two years of a foreign language in high school, while others will be more open to a student who has not studied a foreign language, particularly with an explanation such as a learning disability. However, for certain majors, even the most flexible colleges absolutely require some foreign language credit. It's important to check with the colleges your child is applying to beforehand to ascertain whether or not the school has any foreign language requirement.

•

My child took the SAT with extended time. Will colleges know?

There is no indication on the score report, so colleges will not know unless your child chooses to tell them.

•

My child has a Section 504 Plan and I don't want the colleges to know about it. Is it possible to keep that confidential?

Yes, it is your child's decision whether or not to share this information. Your child's high school cannot share it without a special release, and colleges cannot require disclosure.

• • •

What is financial aid?

Financial aid is supplemental financial support to help you pay for college. You can use your financial aid to pay for both direct costs, such as tuition, fees and room and board, as well as indirect costs like books, travel, supplies and personal expenses related to college attendance. Financial aid includes grants, scholarships, loans and work study.

•

How do we apply for financial aid?

Every student regardless of family income should fill out the FAFSA, the Free Application for Federal Student Aid. The FAFSA will determine your eligibility for federal student aid, such as PELL grants, Federal Direct loans and Federal Work Study. It will also help the college determine your financial need to attend their institution. You complete the FAFSA online at www. fafsa.ed.gov and will have to update the FAFSA for each year that your child is attending college.

•

When do we apply?

You can complete the FAFSA on or after January 1st. The priority deadline for first time college students is between January 15th and February 15th for most schools. Since the deadline is before most people file their taxes, you will have to log back into your FAFSA to update recent tax information after you file. You can use the IRS Data Retrieval Tool, which links directly to the IRS to upload tax information within three weeks of electronic filing. For the CSS Profile you should register at least two weeks before the earliest college priority deadline.

•

But what if I don't have my taxes done in time to get the form submitted by February 15th?

No problem. It is better to do a good close estimate of your financial information and get the application in early than it is to wait until your taxes are done. The key is to do a close estimate.

You can either look at the prior year's taxes and use those as estimates, or you can use the information on the last paystubs from the previous year or from your W2 forms. Once you do your taxes, you simply log in to the FAFSA website and update your information. If your estimates were close, it should not impact your financial aid awards dramatically.

•

What is TAP? (New York State Residents only)

TAP is the Tuition Assistance Program, a state-based grant program for New York residents who attend college within the state and demonstrate need. Students with a family income of $80,000 or below are eligible for TAP. Once you complete the FAFSA, a link to TAP will be provided after submission. Or you could go to www.tap.hesc.ny.gov. Your TAP application will be pre-filled based on the information that you provided on the FAFSA. TAP will only list the first New York state college listed on your FAFSA. After you accept your admissions you can log into your TAP application to change the school.

•

My child is applying for financial aid, but some of my friends' children who are applying to many of the same colleges as my child aren't asking for aid. Will this hurt my child's chances for being admitted?

The vast majority of colleges and universities are "need-blind" in their admissions process. This means that the issue of whether or not a student has financial need does not factor into the college's decision to admit or deny a student. As a matter of fact, the office of admissions and office of financial aid are two separate entities. Each one functions independently of the other. Each student is reviewed individually based on the particular admissions criteria of the college or university, and a person requiring financial assistance and one who does not are at an equal advantage in the process. If a university does use need as one of its admissions criteria, it is required to share that information with the applicant.

•

What is the FAFSA form?

The Free Application for Federal Student Aid is an application created by the federal government to gather critical information about a student's income, assets and, where appropriate, parental income and assets for use in the determination of an estimated family contribution (EFC). The EFC isn't the minimum amount that a student has to pay; it's not the maximum amount that the student has to pay either. As a matter of fact, the student doesn't need to pay it at all. It's just the minimum amount that the federal government says that the student can contribute toward education costs. Each of the colleges that the student lists on the FAFSA form receives this information and uses the EFC to determine what type of financial aid will be offered to the student. The vast majority of colleges and universities require this FAFSA form in order for a student to be considered for any type of federal, state, or institutional aid. It's actually a pretty user-friendly form, with drop down boxes next to each question explaining in more detail what is being requested and where to find it. The form can be found at www.fafsa.gov and remember, it's FREE!

What do I need to complete the FAFSA?

Before completing the FAFSA you will first have to register for a PIN. Your PIN will be used as your electronic signature to submit the FAFSA online. Both you and your child will need a PIN. Only one parent needs to register for a PIN and it can be the same as the student's. To apply, you can go to www.pin.ed.gov. To register, you need your name, date of birth and Social Security number. To complete the FAFSA you should collect the following documents: your driver's license, alien registration number (if applicable) and financial documents for those reporting income. Financial documents include: W2s; federal income tax forms; untaxed income records (Social Security, veteran's benefits, Temporary Assistance for Families); most recent bank statement; and most recent business and investment information.

•

What is considered a "business" for the FAFSA?

The FAFSA identifies a business as having 100 employees or more. If your family's business has fewer than 100 employees, then you enter "0" for the business income.

•

Whose income should be reported on the FAFSA?

Both the student's and the parents' income should be reported on the FAFSA. Even if the student only worked a part time job, it's good practice to start filing taxes as a dependent and report income on the FAFSA. Unless students are making a substantial amount at a summer job, it won't affect eligibility for financial aid. If you as parents are married and live together, then you need to report both parents' incomes. If you are divorced or separated then you report the income of the parent who the student lives with the majority of the time. If a student splits time equally between both parents, then report the income of the parent who provides the most financial support. If a parent is remarried, and is the custodial parent, then a step-parent's income will also need to be provided.

•

What if parents are divorced and a child lives with mom, but is claimed on dad's taxes?

FAFSA only cares about the custodial parent, the parent that provides the most financial support regardless of who claims the child on tax forms.

•

If a parent receives disability payments for a sibling, does that need to be reported on the FAFSA?

No, Social Security disability for a sibling is made in the name of that child and does not count as income for the parent.

•

What is the CSS Profile?

The CSS Profile form is a financial aid application created by the College Board that requests significantly more detail than the federal FAFSA form described above. It can be found on The College Board's website at student.collegeboard.org/css-financial-aid-profile.

For each college that the student sends the report to, a fee is charged, so be sure to determine if a college actually requires the form since only a small percentage of the nation's colleges and universities do. It's a bit more arduous than the FAFSA, and some schools use this information to determine how to award their own institutional need-based aid. The student still must complete the FAFSA.

•

What is a merit-based scholarship? Does it have to be repaid?

Merit-based awards are designed to recognize a student's talent: academic, athletic, artistic, musical or leadership talent. In other words, the student demonstrates a quality that the college or university really values; by awarding free money to the student, the college hopes to encourage enrollment. Merit-based aid is unrelated to financial need. Often, the FAFSA is required before the school will post the awards to a student's financial account, but, remember, these awards are not based on financial need. Be sure to check if the college has an application deadline or any other required steps in order to be considered for these awards. The best part about these scholarships is that they do not need to be repaid. But there may be renewal criteria that the student must meet in order to continue receiving the awards year after year. Read your award letters carefully.

•

What is a need-based award? Does it have to be repaid?

Need-based scholarships are based on either the FAFSA or the FAFSA and some combination of other financial aid applications such as the CSS Profile or institutional forms, the student's Estimated Family Contribution (EFC) and the cost of education at a particular school. Grants do not need to be repaid and can come from the federal government, state government, or the institutions themselves. Some need-based awards don't need to be repaid, but the student has to do something in exchange for the funding, such as the federal work-study program.

There may also be renewal criteria that the student must meet in order to continue receiving the awards year after year. Very important: read your award letters thoroughly.

•

What is the Net Price Calculator?

In response to a federal government mandate, the Net Price Calculator was designed several years ago to provide families with a better and truer estimate of the actual costs of a four- year education at individual institutions. It is an online tool that students and their families can use to get a rough estimate of what the true costs of four years at a given college will be. The student enters self-disclosed, unverified information (including an academic profile and financial circumstances) into the online form, and the calculator generates the estimate. Since the figures are not precise, families should not be overwhelmed by the results. Often, there are additional funds available. It is important to recognize that the report does not guarantee any fixed costs since none of the information submitted by the student is verified.

•

I've heard that unless my family income is very low, there's no point in applying for financial aid. Is that true?

Definitely not! Everyone should fill out the FAFSA form. At the very minimum, a student will learn about eligibility for federal student loans. Maybe you want to take them, maybe you don't... but there is no harm in finding out what's available to you. And in many cases, even those families who think they won't qualify for any aid are surprised at what the institutions will offer. You need to give the colleges a reason to evaluate your family for assistance, and filling out the FAFSA is the perfect way to do that.

•

What financial aid forms must be filled out?

At the very minimum, the FAFSA form should be completed by all students. In certain circumstances, there are additional forms, such as state applications for aid and institutional forms that may be required. Students should check with each school they are applying to in order to find out for sure.

•

My spouse and I are divorced. Will that impact my child getting financial aid?

When a student is considered a dependent student in the eyes of the federal government, the marital status of the student's parents does impact eligibility for financial aid. When filing the FAFSA, the student will be asked to indicate the marital status of his/her parents. In the event that both parents are still married to each other, the income and assets for both parents gets included on the FAFSA. In the event of a divorce or separation, the custodial parent must be identified. Let's say that's Mom. Mom's income and assets would appear on the form, and ex-husband Dad's income and assets would not appear anywhere on the form. The form does have a line for listing child support and household support, but the non-custodial parent's income and assets are not required on the FAFSA form. It gets a bit tricky if the custodial parent gets re-married. When the custodial parent's marital status is married, both the custodial parent and step-parent's income and assets appear on the FAFSA form. The CSS Profile form and some institutional supplemental forms will also require information about the non-custodial parent, but the FAFSA does not.

•

When do we find out if we're eligible for any aid?

A college or university cannot make an official offer of financial aid to a student until that student has been admitted to the institution. In some cases, you will be applying for financial aid, listing a particular college on the FAFSA form, and submitting the information before you know if your child has been accepted. The colleges cannot import the information from the FAFSA form into their systems until an acceptance has been offered. But as soon as it has been done, the college will process your financial information and prepare a financial aid award letter that details all the various types of aid that the student is eligible to receive, the cost to attend and a list of next steps. Depending on the size of the institution, this can take anywhere from 2-6 weeks from the time a student has been admitted to the college and all financial aid applications have been filed.

•

Should I be negotiating with the colleges to try to get more aid?

Generally speaking, colleges and universities put their best foot forward right from the very beginning when it comes to offering financial aid to students. It's in the school's best interest to be as affordable as possible, so they tend to offer as much as possible from the very beginning. That said, both people and computers make mistakes. So if you believe you have not received funding that you are entitled to, you can certainly contact the financial aid office and inquire about your eligibility. Sometimes a college may have a small number of scholarships available to assist students who are very close to being able to make it work financially, so asking can't hurt; it's just not likely that big gaps will be able to be closed through this process. Also, be sure to make the college aware of any extenuating circumstances.

•

We can only list 10 schools on the FAFSA; what if my child is applying to more schools?

If applying to more than 10 schools, then list the first ten schools and submit. Once the FAFSA has been processed, within three days, your family will receive your Student Aid Report (SAR). After receiving your SAR, you can log back into your application, erase the schools initially listed and submit any additional schools.

•

What is the difference between subsidized and unsubsidized loans?

Subsidized loans are loans in which the government pays the interest on your loan while students are in school. Unsubsidized loans are loans in which interest accrues while students are still in school. Unsubsidized loans have quarterly statements, and offer the option to pay the interest at that time or capitalize the interest to the principle, meaning that the interest will be added to the total amount of the original loan.

•

What is Work Study?

Work Study is a federal student aid program in which students get a job on campus and receive a paycheck for the hours worked. Work Study is not guaranteed. It depends on the availability of jobs on campus. The money received from working goes directly to students and can be used for personal expenses while in school. If Work Study is part of a package, then your child should go to the financial aid office when first arriving on campus to secure a job placement.

•

What if my child receives an outside scholarship, do we need to report it to the college?

Yes, if a student receives a scholarship outside of the financial aid package from the school then it must be reported to the school. The school can do one of three things: reduce the amount of institutional aid given, reduce the amount of loans offered, or make no changes to the financial aid package. Most of the time schools will either make no changes or reduce the amount of loans offered.

•

What if we don't want to take out loans or we don't want to take out the full amount?

The loan portion of a financial aid package is an offer that you have to accept, not an automatic given like grants. You don't necessarily need to accept the full amount if your family could afford not to. However, the majority of students need to take out student loans to help support them through college. When evaluating your financial aid package you need to consider your financial responsibility for the first year in addition to your financial responsibility for the full four years of attendance. Keep in mind that federal student loans have a low interest rate in addition to a variety of repayment options.

•

Should my child indicate on the application that we will be applying for financial aid? I heard this can be a disadvantage in admissions.

Many colleges used to be 100% "need blind," which means that applying for admission and being accepted had nothing to do with getting financial aid. Now, a number of schools are "need aware," which means that when it's down to the wire between accepting a student who can pay the full price and one who can't, the student who does not need financial aid can be at an advantage. Always check with the Financial Aid office of the school if you have any questions about the aid process.

•

What if the financial aid package doesn't cover the full cost of attendance?

When evaluating financial aid packages you want to look at who presents the best offer. Several factors play into the evaluation of your package. The total cost of attendance minus your Estimated Family Contribution equals your financial need. Your financial need minus your financial aid package equals your gap. Your gap is the amount of money that will have to be paid out-of-pocket to attend the school.

If the gap is too much, then it might make sense to reconsider options. Or you may be able to take out more in Parent Plus loans. Parent Plus loans are loans for parents to take out to help supplement financial aid packages.

•

What are Extenuating Circumstances and how should I let the Financial Aid Office know about them?

If anything occurs concerning your financial situation after you submit applications (loss of job, loss of business, large medical expenses, etc.) or if there is something significant about your financial situation which cannot be reflected on forms, you need to contact the Financial Aid Office of each school. They will usually ask you to write a letter explaining these "Extenuating Circumstances." Your financial aid package may be adjusted as a result.

• • •

Why should my children go to a US university?

With over 4,000 institutions and some of the best universities in the world, higher education in the US offers the chance to experience a world-class, liberal arts education. US universities have rich campus climates and outstanding facilities, which students can take advantage of through resources such as extracurricular activities, internships and research. Studying abroad gives students the chance to experience a new culture and internationalize their curriculum vitae (CV), something which employers value in prospective employees. US institutions also offer excellent advising and mentorship to help students create communities for themselves and achieve academic and personal success.

•

What does "Liberal Arts" mean?

A "Liberal Arts" education emphasizes breadth in addition to depth in academic pursuits. Students will have the chance to study a variety of subjects in addition to their chosen field of specialization. For many international students, the "Liberal Arts" education is the reason they are attracted to US universities because it allows them to explore all of their academic interests. If your child is undecided as to what to study, this structure may be a good option. Not all US universities follow this model, so be sure to do your research.

•

Are international students expected to score at the same level as US students on the SAT or ACT?

Admissions officers will be aware that children who do not attend an American school will most likely be unfamiliar with standardized tests like the SAT or ACT. Since evaluation of an application is holistic, they will keep this in mind when reviewing and comparing it to American applicants. However, some selective schools will expect high scores from all applicants so it is important to study for admissions tests.

•

If my child is applying to universities in our own country, how many US university applications should be submitted?

There is no limit to the number of US universities to which your child can apply. However, each application may require substantial work. Applying to universities in your own country, as well as completing approximately 5-7 US university applications, will create options without becoming overwhelming. If only applying to US universities, many students will apply to 10-12 institutions. It's essential to develop an application strategy across all the universities to insure a range of options from 'reach' to 'safety'.

•

Will taking a gap year affect an application to US universities?

If your child is currently taking a gap year, make sure to keep in touch with the school so that it can prepare the school documents necessary for an application. If applying and then deferring an acceptance, it is best to find out the individual policies for each university. Often universities will want to know why students want to defer, and whether they are doing something worthwhile, so be prepared to explain a plan for a gap year. Gap years are more common for US students these days and universities can look on them favorably if it makes good use of the time: work, volunteering, or learning a language can be valuable experiences.

•

Do US universities prefer the IB/A levels/Bac or something else?

Most universities will have no preference and are familiar with international qualifications. Admissions officers may be less knowledgeable of some of the nuances of a particular system or school (e.g. whether students take 3 or 4 A2s or the difference between an A and A*). If necessary, school officials may include explanatory information when generating your child's transcript. One factor to consider is that as a more broad-based curriculum the IB is perhaps more similar to coursework at a US university.

•

Can I use my UCAS essay for the Personal Statement?

Students should not use their UCAS essay for an American personal statement since both essays have different purposes. While a UCAS essay should reflect why your child is interested in studying a particular subject, an American personal statement should reflect something more personal: character, interests, experiences and values. Essentially, an American admissions officer wants to gain a more complete picture of an applicant and so it requires your child to go beyond the academic, specific focus of the UCAS essay.

•

How do US universities rank compared to universities in my country?

The US has some of the best universities in the world. In fact, the Times World University Rankings 2016 found that 17 of the top 25 universities in the world were located in the US. Often international students are more familiar with the historically most prestigious US institutions, but it is essential to look beyond the brand names, do your research and select the universities that will fit best. Rankings can be a useful method to help inform the college search but should not be based on them alone!

•

Is there financial aid for international students?

Yes, but it is limited! Over 180 universities offer financial aid to international students through a variety of grants, scholarships and loans. Applications for financial aid should be completed at the same time as an application for admission. It is important to research whether a university offers international financial aid before applying. Each university will have a specific calculation to assess whether your family is eligible for financial aid and if so, at what level. Outstanding athletes may also qualify for sports scholarships—www. ncaa.org is a good place to start.

•

What is a GPA? What is a transcript?

A transcript is a record of academic grades for the last four years of secondary school. This is a required part of most university applications and should be prepared by a school official on school letterhead. GPA stands for 'grade point average' which is a calculated average of final grades for most or all subjects. If your child's school does not use a GPA system, that is fine, and admissions officers will evaluate academic performance based on transcript, school report and teacher recommendations.

•

None or only one of the subjects my child studies is offered as an SAT Subject Test. What should we do?

In this case, the Math I or the English Literature Subject Test may be good options since students are likely to have some background in these subjects. This background should be supplemented with extra studying. Another option is to take US or World History, but this may require significant preparation. The best approach is to review the curriculum, take a practice test and make an informed decision as to which test will suit best. It's important to confirm the test dates when Subject Tests are offered (World History is only offered in December and June).

•

Can my child take an SAT Subject Test in our native language?

Most schools would prefer that students do not take a SAT Subject Test in their native language since they want to see ability in a subject acquired through study. However, it is best to check with individual universities to see if they have a preference. Also, if English is not your children's first language the TOEFL or IELTS may be required.

•

Can my child study medicine or law as an undergraduate in the US?

No, these are post-graduate courses and students must complete an undergraduate degree before studying law or medicine. Some universities offer pre-law or pre-medicine tracks of study to help prepare students for medical and law degrees, but these degrees do not qualify your child to practice law or medicine. It is important to note that admission to medical school for international students can be extremely difficult and financial aid is rarely available.

•

What does an admissions officer look for in an international application?

Most schools have a holistic process of admission. Of course, academic abilities are extremely important, but an admissions officer will also take into account factors such as extracurricular involvement, interest in the school, personal attributes and diverse experiences and perspectives. Not only do they like to see what a student would gain from studying at their institution, but also what that student can contribute to the student community at the school. Therefore, it is critical that the various elements of an application present the full range and depth of a student's interests.

• • •

—— Some Final Words of Wisdom ——
"Must Do's" for Parents

How can I best support my child throughout the college process?

Encourage your child to be proactive; he/she must take charge of the college process. Colleges expect it, and this will be an important factor in college admissions.

a. Your child must complete his/her application, send their testing to schools, do the research, set up the college visits, ask the questions and definitely be the one emailing the admissions representatives.

b. Your child must keep track of deadlines, know what materials need to be sent and check all college accounts and emails from colleges. Yes, there's a great deal of work to be done after all applications/materials are submitted. Many colleges will ask students to set up accounts to check the status of their application and make sure that all materials have been received. It takes time for schools to upload transcripts and recommendations into their systems so an account may indicate something is missing when it is there but simply not entered. It is the student's responsibility to periodically check his/her accounts and inform their school counselor. Sometimes materials need to be re-sent.

c. Since Common Application essay topics are released in the spring, your child should work on his/her essay and resume and have them completed and proofread before they leave for summer vacation. When the Common Application goes live on August 1 and your child registers for an account and starts to fill out his/her application, with the finalized essay and resume behind them, a big chunk has already been done.

You may feel overwhelmed, confused, frustrated and wanting so much to support your child; do not fall into the situation of doing everything for them. Do everything you can to help him/ her to be proactive. You will feel better and so will your child.

• • •

Why is it so difficult letting go?

In a moment filled with joy, there is still an element of sadness, when after occupying your home and your heart for 18 years, children leave for college. But leave they must. As Dr. Jonas Salk once said, "Good parents give their children Roots and Wings. Roots to know where home is, Wings to fly away and exercise what's been taught them." Take heart in knowing that your children will take with them on their new journey everything they learned from you over the course of those 18 years. It's okay to feel sad, but it's also okay to feel proud.

•

Will I only see my child during vacations?

Most parents will get to see their children during the summer months as well as during Thanksgiving, Christmas/Hanukkah and Easter/Passover vacations. Additionally, some colleges have fall and spring breaks, which typically give students about five days off in October and again in February or March. Furthermore, students may pursue options during school breaks including internship opportunities which may mean longer periods of not seeing one another. Remember, there are plenty of ways to visually connect with your child when college is in session, including Skype and FaceTime.

•

How much will leaving for college change the family dynamics?

While all families will feel the impact of a child leaving the nest, how much the dynamics will change depends on the family, including family size and closeness. The impact will typically be most keenly felt by families of only children and those who have been very connected to their children throughout their lives. One more thought: While it is normal to want to stay in regular contact with your child during college, it is also important to give them the opportunity to live his or her own life. By letting go, you are giving your child the freedom to move forward.

•

My child doesn't graduate for another year (or two or three!), and yet I'm already starting to feel sad and anxious. Is this normal?

It is not only normal; it's natural. It's called anticipatory anxiety, and it refers to the impending sadness you're beginning to feel when your child leaves home. Your child will likely experience the same feelings and might begin to exhibit these feelings in unsettling and unexpected ways, including arguing with you, and showing less patience. While all of this emotional upheaval is typical and even predictable, it probably won't feel at all familiar to you—at least not with the first child you send off to college.

The two lasting gifts we can give our children are roots and wings. They will be fine and so will you!

• • •

- *The Book of Knowledge SAT (Redesigned Test)*
  Everything you need for the SAT

- *The Book of Knowledge SAT Student Solutions (Redesigned Test)*
  Detailed explanations for the SAT book

- *The Book of Knowledge SAT Teacher Manual*
  All of the regular book alongside explanations

- *The Vocabulary Box*
  500 essential SAT, ACT and high school vocabulary words; available as a box of flashcards or a workbook

- *Vocab Videos Flashcards*
  A companion to the Vocab Videos site Available as a box of flashcards or a workbook

- *The Book of Knowledge ACT*
  Everything you need for the ACT

- *The Book of Knowledge ACT Student Solutions*
  Detailed explanations for the ACT book

- *The Book of Knowledge ACT Teacher Manual*
  All of the regular book alongside explanations

VOCAB VIDEOS

Bringing Vocabulary to Life

WWW.VOCABVIDEOS.COM

- Hilarious short videos illustrate the meanings of 500 high value, frequently-tested SAT, ACT, & high school vocabulary words.

- Features entertaining characters, outrageous plotlines, and parodies of your favorite TV shows and movies.

- Contains extensive online review material including:

  - Quizzes for each episode

  - Worksheets to write sentences and mnemonic devices

  - Multimedia flashcard maker: create flashcards for any academic subjects (you can even upload your own images and videos!)

  - Downloadable crossword puzzles for a fun review

Sample Flashcard

- *NEW* photo and video uploading functionality allows students to create their own vocab photos and videos!

Get started at www.VocabVideos.com.

Enter coupon code BOK6 in Step 3 of Checkout to receive 25% off

college essay organizer
All your essay questions in one place

Our groundbreaking admissions technology – your secret weapon

We do all the hard work so you don't have to. Used by the top schools from New York to South Korea, our easy-to-use web tool will make sure you:

- **Save hours** researching essay questions and putting together a writing plan

- **Avoid overlooking key essay questions,** especially for departments, programs, and scholarships that are shockingly not listed on the Common App or the school applications

- **Get the new essay questions as soon as they are posted (or sooner)** with our instant notification system

- **Write fewer essays** by seeing how all your different questions overlap by topic

HOW TO GET STARTED FOR FREE

Go to **CollegeEssayOrganizer.com** and click "Start Here" on the top right. Simply select your colleges to get your essay questions all in one place — *instantly.*

To upgrade to a premium account, use the promo code **answers** for 50% off. **More than 90% of members who upgraded were accepted to their #1 choice colleges.**

www.CollegeEssayOrganizer.com

info@CollegeEssayOrganizer.com

646.448.4927

CPSIA information can be obtained
at www.ICGtesting.com
Printed in the USA
FFOW05n1659280316